CW00407253

CHELTENHAM RACES

RACES

P E T E R   G I L L

SUTTON PUBLISHING LIMITED

Sutton Publishing Limited
Phoenix Mill · Thrupp · Stroud
Gloucestershire · GL5 2BU

First published 1997

Copyright © Peter Gill, 1997

Title page: *Golden Miller* and *Thomond II* neck
and neck in the 1935 Gold Cup.

British Library Cataloguing in Publication Data
A catalogue record for this book is available from the
British Library.

ISBN 0-7509-1550-1

Typeset in 10/12 Perpetua.
Typesetting and origination by
Sutton Publishing Limited.
Printed in Great Britain by
Ebenezer Baylis, Worcester.

This book is dedicated to my wife Jayne who gave me a dream.
And to Ethan who is that dream.

The Cheltenham Jockeys Cricket Team, early 1930s. Back row, left to right: ? Newall, W. White,
G. Pullen, G.S. Wood, T.F. Rimell and F. Taylor. Front row: Umpire, D. Jones, Tim Hamey with Rex
Hamey, W. Speck, G. Wilson with John Hamey, Eric Foster and E. Driscoll.

CONTENTS

Outside the weighing room at Cheltenham, 1930s. Many of the jump racing jockeys of the period are present for this photograph, some still wearing their racing colours.

INTRODUCTION

Around 1718 it was noticed by some observant citizens of Cheltenham that pigeons patronized a salts deposit left by a small spring that flowed through the thick clay of Bayshill. The spring surfaced in a field which is now the site of the Princess Hall in Cheltenham Ladies' College. These pigeons were in subsequent years acknowledged by being included upon the Cheltenham coat of arms, and today visitors to the town can see their effigies perched upon many of the signposts in the town centre. It is quite possible that without these pigeons Cheltenham would never have developed to become as prosperous and as large a town as it is today and, more than likely, would never have become the home to National Hunt Racing.

Noticing these pigeons enjoying the natural minerals, William Mason sunk a small well near the spring and for a few years kept it open for anyone wishing to partake of these natural waters. After a while it became necessary to enclose the well as its popularity increased, but little more happened until 1738 when Henry Skillicorne, the son-in-law of William Mason, inherited the well and some property around it. He moved from Bristol, where he had served the Elton family as a merchant sea captain, to Cheltenham. His first innovation was to deepen the well and construct a pumping system.

In 1740 Dr Short wrote, in his *History of Mineral Waters*, that upon much research he believed the natural waters of Cheltenham to be superior to any others in the country. This statement did much to promote the importance of the town, but it was not until 1788 that the destiny of the town was assured. In that year the popular but ailing King George III and his entourage paid a five-week visit to the town to experience the famous 'healing' waters. Most days the King would drink a glass of water from Skillicorne's well (later known as The Royal Well, or King's Well) and then enjoy the offerings of the town and its environs.

This royal visit had the effect of elevating Cheltenham to a town of great fashionable importance, both at the time of the visit and during the ensuing years. By the turn of the century, when the population of the town stood at just over 3,000, approximately 2,000 people were visiting the town annually. Spas began to spring up all over the town as various entrepreneurs sought to cash in on the demand for the Cheltenham waters. Lodging-houses were built to house the tourists and much work was done to develop the roads and walks of the town. Roads to Bath, Birmingham and Gloucester were built to provide vital links to the rest of the country, links that would nurture the town through its difficult infancy.

Into this developing scene, under the initial patronage of the Duke of Gloucester, eased a sporting pastime that would cling to the town and yet struggle for popularity in such a way that for almost a century it would stutter between success and failure until it finally exploded into life, such that today it is as much a part of Cheltenham as Cheltenham is a part of the sport. The sport was, and is, horse-racing.

If in the early nineteenth century Cheltenham was nationally famous for its waters, then in the twentieth century it is internationally known for its National Hunt Racing. In a town where hoards once gathered to taste the waters that had been tasted by royalty, today they gather to celebrate with royalty a sport that has truly found a home. When once it was impressive to seduce 2,000 people annually to the town to drink the waters, today close on a quarter of a million people pass through the turnstiles of the Prestbury Park Racecourse during the sixteen days of racing held there each year. For at least three days of the year, during the March National Hunt Festival, Cheltenham is completely overwhelmed by the influx of race enthusiasts, particularly those from the Emerald Isle. No bed goes spare in any of the town's hotels. The town's shops, pubs and restaurants attempt to attract the racegoers with window displays and entertainments.

The Cheltenham Promenade as the early racegoers would have recognized it. These Regency villas were built in the early 1820s along with much of The Promenade. The land was previously a swampy area known as the Lord's Meadow. The tree-lined Promenade led to the Imperial Spa (now the site of the Queen's Hotel) and to the Montpellier Spa (now Lloyds Bank).

The Promenade and its Regency villas today. Five of the original villas were bought for use as Municipal Offices in 1915. Much of the rest of The Promenade would be unrecognizable for a nineteenth-century racegoer.

The atmosphere of the Festival can be felt throughout Cheltenham, but there is rarely any trouble and even the inevitable traffic congestion symptomatic of such an event in the modern world is largely accepted as par for the course by the town's citizens. The Races have adopted the town and the town has adopted the Races. A housing estate bears the names of some of the most legendary names that have trod the turf in Cheltenham and several pubs in the town bear homage to mighty winners by taking their names.

Horse racing at Cheltenham has always been a sport that has appealed to people from all walks of life. Prosperous or not the sport welcomes you to enjoy the occasion, the atmosphere and the event. For almost two hundred years it has been enjoyed in Cheltenham and a number of horses and trainers who have found success have become household names: *Golden Miller*, *Arkle*, *Dawn Run*, *Desert Orchid*, Pat Taaffe, Fred Winter, Fred and Mercy Rimell and Fulke Walwyn to name but a few. Some of these names were famous only during their period of success, but some have developed into names of almost mythical proportions.

Cheltenham Races seem set to produce countless new names, stories and images over future years that will doubtless equal the legends that have already stamped their mark on the town; perhaps, in some instances, they might surpass them. This book illustrates the history of the Races at Cheltenham from the crude beginnings in the early eighteenth century to the incredible sophistication of today. Many of the horses and personalities that have made Cheltenham Races what they are are pictured here, many more are recalled in text. Overall it is hoped that this book will bring the history and atmosphere of the Races to life, to be enjoyed equally by those who have lived and breathed horse racing all their life and by those who may just have a passing interest in the sport or in the town.

This book also aims to pay homage to the heroes and heroines, both human and equine, that have made Cheltenham the home, both spiritually and physically, of National Hunt Racing.

Peter Gill,
May 1997.

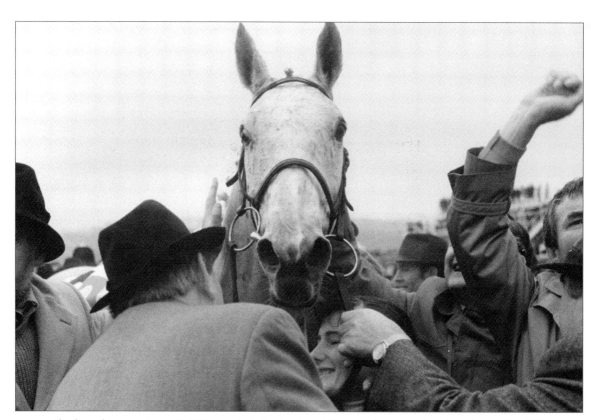

The face of success: *Desert Orchid*, one of Cheltenham's and horse racing's legends, after winning the 1989 Gold Cup.

FROM SMALL BEGINNINGS . . .

The first properly organized Cheltenham race meeting seems to have been that held on Nottingham Hill in 1815, although racing had been held near Cheltenham for several years – in particular on Tewkesbury Ham and Minchinhampton Common. The 1815 race meet was not a great success and it was three years before the plunge was taken again to organize a proper meet. This occurred on Tuesday 25 August 1818 on Cleeve Hill. Mr E. Jones of the Shakespeare Inn in the lower High Street organized the affair and it was his five-year-old brown mare, *Miss Tidmarsh*, that became the first recorded winner of the Cheltenham Races. These were still the days before hurdles and fences and the race she won was a mile-long flat race.

The Races were deemed such a success that it was proposed they should become an annual event for the town and that a racecourse should be set out and a grandstand constructed on the hill. The Duke of Gloucester became the first patron of Cheltenham Races, subscribing 100 guineas.

A course was duly set out on the West Down of Cleeve Hill and, amid great local publicity, a three-day meeting was held between 23 and 25 August 1819. There were two major races, the Gloucestershire Stakes held on 23 August over a distance of 2 miles, which was won by *Champignon* owned by a Mr Calley, and the first ever Cheltenham Gold Cup held on 24 August, a weight for age flat race held over a distance of 3 miles which was won by *Spectre* owned by Mr Bodenham; *Spectre* had finished second to *Champignon* the previous day. The prize for that first Gold Cup was 100 guineas.

The grandstand erected on Cleeve Common was by all accounts impressive and some reports indicate that it could be seen from the Cheltenham Promenade – it was probably on the site now occupied by the pylons at the western end of West Down.

From then on the Races began to flourish. By 1825 crowds were estimated at 50,000, all of whom could be entertained by the numerous events held in the town as well as on the Racecourse where there were stalls selling all manner of wares, sideshows and the all important gambling booths. Inevitably, with such large crowds, the criminal element was attracted and pickpockets were the scourge of nineteenth-century racegoers just as they are today.

The initial success was so great that better roads had to be organized. Instead of all racegoers coming through Prestbury and up what is now Mill Lane to the hill, it was advised in 1826 that racegoers should use the 'new' London Road and come to the Racecourse via Whittington.

Cheltenham at this time was in a transitional period and was receiving some bad press nationally. Still living off its Royal visit of nearly forty years ago, it was now seen as a hedonistic and self-gratifying town – the Races and their attached gambling and partying did nothing to dispel this belief. Into this arena came the Revd Francis Close, a young, strong and charismatic orator who, from his pulpit in the parish church, preached sermons against the evils of horse racing that were later printed and sold in their thousands. He aroused the emotions of his congregation to such an extent that in 1829 the race meeting was disrupted by mobs shouting abuse and hurling stones and other objects at the horses and their riders. In 1830 the grandstand was burnt to the ground.

At this juncture the Races might have completely folded if it had not been for a previous arrangement to use Prestbury Park. Back in 1823 a yeoman of Prestbury, Thomas Robinson, who had leased part of Prestbury Park from its owner, Keppel Craven, Lord of Prestbury Manor, signed an agreement with J.D. Kelly (owner of the town's Assembly Rooms and one of the original supporters of Cheltenham Races) whereby the Race Committee could have use of three fields for one week in every year in June and July. Since the Races were successful on Cleeve Hill this agreement was not initially acted upon, but after the evangelical movement against the Races a meeting was held for the first time at Prestbury Park in 1831.

It has been widely reported that it was Lord Ellenborough, the Governor of India from 1841 to 1844, who came to the rescue of the Cheltenham Races in 1830 and that it was he who owned Prestbury Park and allowed it to be used for racing. This belief probably originates from the fact that Ellenborough bought Southam DelaBere in 1839 and it was assumed that Prestbury Park belonged to this Tudor manor house. In actual fact Prestbury Park was owned by the Craven family from 1622, when they bought the manorial rights, until 1853, when both the park and the manor were sold. On today's Ordnance Survey maps the site of the old Prestbury Manor can still be seen on the eastern side of the Racecourse, marked 'Moat' (this is at the end of Park Lane in Prestbury). It had been an impressive, moated building with a drawbridge and perfectly sited for access to the acreage of Prestbury Park.

For that first Prestbury Park race meeting a 700-capacity grandstand was erected and because of the better accessibility it was hoped that the races would continue to flourish. On 19 July 1831 the first winner at Prestbury Park was *Confederacy* in the Gloucestershire Stakes. Three years later in 1834, while flat racing was still being run at Prestbury Park where Fulwar Craven was one of the stewards, J. Ballinger clerk of the course and W.W. Bryer secretary, the first steeplechase was inaugurated as part of Cheltenham Races, but at Andoversford. This steeplechase was run on Friday 4 April, there having been flat racing at Prestbury Park on the Thursday, and it was won by Mr D'Oyley on his own horse *Fugleman;* subsequently this race would become known as the Cheltenham Grand Annual Steeplechase.

The turf at Prestbury Park was not as good as that on the hill and in 1835 the Races returned to Cleeve Hill where a three-storey grandstand was built and the Whittington Road to the hill was improved. Within seven years, however, flat racing at Cheltenham was dying, meetings were badly attended and the whole glamour that initially surrounded it had evaporated. The mood of the town had become more sober, thanks in no small part to Francis Close, but also because of the nationwide economic depression. The standard of racing on the hill had deteriorated and even a renaming of the races in 1840 as 'The County of Gloucester Races on Cleeve Hill Course' failed to save the sport. Apart from a final meeting in June 1855, flat racing on Cleeve Hill and in Cheltenham died.

However, just as interest in flat racing diminished, steeplechasing began to become more popular. The 1834 steeplechase became an annual race, and on 14 April 1847 it moved back to Prestbury on a course mapped out by Col. Berkeley stretching from Knoll Hill House to The Hewletts via Noverton Farm. The race was won by William Holman on *Stanmore* with William Archer finishing second on *Daddy Longlegs*. This race was immortalized in Adam Lindsay Gordon's poem 'How we Beat the Favourite'.

The race continued to be held in Prestbury Park until the land was sold in 1853 for £19,600. The new owner was totally opposed to racing and would not have it on his land. So, for several years the Grand Annual was nomadic. At first it moved to Bibury, in 1856 it was run on the old Gloucester Road in Cheltenham and in 1857 at Andoversford. Kayte Farm in Southam became a temporary home until the grandstand there collapsed in 1866 and the race organizers were sued for £2,500.

As the century drew to a close, racing of all kinds was losing popularity and Cheltenham Races seemed destined to die a quiet death, but in 1881 Prestbury Park was sold by C.N. Dodson to Mr W. Baring Bingham, a racing enthusiast who wanted to revive its former glories.

A painting of the 1826 Gloucestershire Stakes flat race held on Cleeve Hill on Wednesday 19 July won by Mr Yates' *Cain* from Mr Browne's *Burgundy*. This is quite possibly the only picture of the Races when they were held on the hill. Also in 1826 Francis Close was appointed vicar of St Mary's, Cheltenham's parish church. (*reproduction courtesy of Cheltenham Art Gallery and Museum*)

A portrait of Francis Close painted in about 1850. He was born on 11 July 1797 and moved to Cheltenham in 1824 to become curate at Holy Trinity Church. His attacks on Cheltenham Races became more powerful and gained in momentum when he moved to St Mary's where he stayed some thirty years. He became Dean of Carlisle in 1856 and died in Cornwall on 18 December 1882 having lived a long, active and influential life.

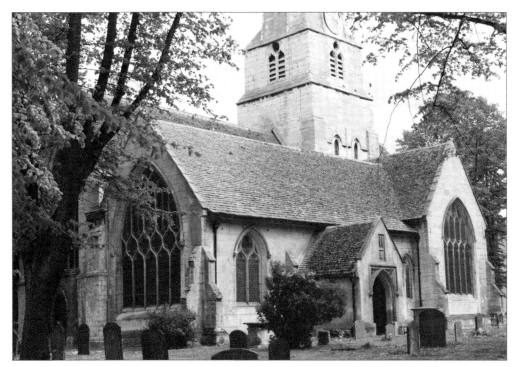

Cheltenham's parish church, St Mary's, from where the Revd Francis Close delivered his most scathing sermons on the evils of horse racing. Francis Close was a born orator and his sermons were aimed to incite reaction. In 1829 members of his congregation attempted to disrupt the race meeting on the hill and it is widely believed that his parishioners were responsible for burning down the Cleeve Hill grandstand in 1830.

The Whittington road to the Racecourse on West Down, Cleeve Hill. This road was improved for the return of the Races to the hill in 1835 and was the main approach to the course for visitors coming off the Cheltenham–London road to Whittington.

Kayte Farm in Southam Lane, Southam, the venue for several Cheltenham race meetings in the mid-nineteenth century. It was here that a grandstand was erected and later collapsed with spectators crashing into the refreshment room below. This grandstand was probably located on the site where the Smiths Industries' sports pavilion now stands.

The boyhood home of Adam Lindsay Gordon, 28 Carlton Street, Cheltenham. Born at Fayal in the Azores on 19 October 1833, Gordon was one of the first boys to attend Cheltenham College when it was founded in July 1841; his father was Professor of Oriental Languages there. He left in June 1842, but after a private tutor and the Royal Military Academy at Woolwich gave up on him (he was thrown out of Woolwich for stealing a horse to ride in a race which he won!) he returned to Cheltenham College in 1850 for a short period. He was introduced to horse racing at the age of fifteen when a livery-keeper named George Reeves began to give him lessons. 'Black' Tom Oliver, thrice winner of the Grand National who was also tutoring George Stevens at the time, then took him under his wing, gave him some rides as an amateur and also introduced him to boxing which he began to practise in local pubs. He regularly took rides in the area and later wrote the poem, 'How we Beat the Favourite', based on the 1847 Cheltenham Grand Annual Steeplechase won by William Holman on *Stanmore*. In the poem Gordon imagines himself as the winner of the race on a mare named *Iseult*, beating George Stevens on *The Clown*.

Adam Lindsay Gordon at the age of thirty. He was too interested in sports, namely horse racing and boxing, for the academic life his father planned for him and was eventually sent away to Australia where he became an MP and the National Poet.

Lindsay Gordon in his racing colours – the tilt of the cap was characteristic of the man. In Australia he became champion amateur jockey and never gave up racing. Tragically he took his own life, shooting himself on 23 June 1870. A contemporary and friend of Gordon at Cheltenham College was Tom Pickernell who rode under the pseudonym of Mr Thomas because his family did not approve. Tom Pickernell went on to win three Grand Nationals.

Emblem Cottage at the top of Stockwell Lane on Cleeve Hill, the home of George Stevens, who named it after the horse he rode to success in the 1863 Grand National. George Stevens was born in 1833 and learnt his riding technique from 'Black' Tom Oliver – a real Cheltenham legend. At Emblem Cottage he trained a few racehorses from 1866 but was tragically killed in a riding accident in 1871.

George Stevens on *Emblem* with the horse's owner, Lord Coventry. As well as winning the 1863 Grand National, *Emblem* won the Cheltenham Grand Annual Steeplechase in 1863 and 1865; he was trained by E. Weever. George Stevens first won the Grand National on the William Holman-trained *Freetrader* in 1856 and in 1864 he won his third National on Lord Coventry's *Emblematic*, again trained by E. Weever.

George Stevens still holds the record for the number of winning rides in the National. In 1869 he made it four on *The Colonel* and in 1870, on the same horse, he made it five. Each time he won the race bonfires were lit at the top of Cleeve Hill in celebration of the achievement. In 1871 he rode *The Colonel* to win the Victuallers' Plate at Cheltenham Races, his last win. He was returning from a trip to Cheltenham market on his hack *The Clown* when the horse bolted down the hill, alarmed by a gust of wind that blew off Stevens' hat. It tripped on an exposed drainpipe and George Stevens, who had never suffered any serious injury during his twenty-year riding career, was thrown from the horse just outside Villars Farm. He was taken into the home of Mrs Villars, but his injuries were fatal.

The plaque in Southam, at the base of Cleeve Hill, in memory of George Stevens who was killed on that spot in June 1871 at the tender age of thirty-eight.

This plaque outside the King's Arms in Prestbury announces that it was here, while his father was landlord, that Fred Archer trained upon a diet of toast, water and coffee. Fred Archer was actually born at St George's Cottages in Cheltenham on 11 January 1857, but the family moved to Prestbury soon after, initially to Cintra House and then later that year to the King's Arms.

At this Prestbury Inn lived
FRED ARCHER the jockey
Who trained upon toast,
Cheltenham water & coffee
The shoe of his pony
hangs in the Bar
where they drink to his prowess
from near and from far
But the man in the street
passes by without knowledge
that tu'as here Archer
swallowed his earliest porridge

The King's Arms in Prestbury, the childhood home of the thirteen-time (in consecutive years) Champion Jockey, Fred Archer. Fred's father, William, had been stud manager to Tsar Nicholas I in Russia but returned to England and married Emma Hayward, the daughter of the licensee of the King's Arms, where he subsequently became landlord. William won the 1858 Grand National on William Holman's *Little Charley* and the pub became a regular meeting-place for the racing fraternity. All three of his sons rode; William junior was killed at Cheltenham in 1878 when he fell in a hurdle race and Charles was the winner of the Cheltenham Grand Annual in the same year.

A portrait of Fred Archer as Champion Jockey, a feat he accomplished at the age of seventeen, having ridden his first winner at twelve. Whereas his brothers were jump jockeys, Fred rode on the flat, a much more popular sport at that time. His incredible horsemanship brought him great fame and his marriage to Helen Rose Dawson on 31 January 1883 was the main social event of the year in Newmarket, such was his standing.

However, his few years were tragic ones and the troubles he suffered must have contributed to his suicide at the age of twenty-nine on 8 November 1886, when he shot himself in a severe state of typhoid-induced depression. In January 1884 his first child, a son, died after just a few hours, and in November of the same year his wife died shortly after giving birth to a daughter.

In a short but brilliant career Fred Archer set the racing world alight. Between 1870 and his death in 1886 he rode 8,004 races of which he won 2,148; he twice won on all six of his mounts on seven-race cards, at Newmarket on 19 April 1877 and at Lewes on 5 August 1882; and in 1885 he rode 246 winners. He won the Derby five times, the 2000 Guineas four times, the 1000 Guineas twice, the Oaks four times and the St Leger six times.

THE HOLMAN/NICHOLSON DYNASTY

Shortly after marrying Eliza Ward in London in 1833, William Holman moved with his bride to Cheltenham to set up business as a shoemaker. His first son, also named William, was born in 1835 and so began a racing dynasty that has lasted up to the present day, with the great-great-grandson of the original William Holman being Champion Racehorse Trainer, David Nicholson. The Holman/Nicholson dynasty developed alongside racing at Cheltenham, and has played a greater part in its history than any other family.

William and Eliza Holman eventually had six sons and three daughters to carry their line, but it was William senior who began the horse racing success story, when at the age of thirty he came third on a horse named *Manfred*, owned by a Mr Hassey, in a race held on 19 February 1841 from The Hewletts in Prestbury to Andoversford. On 30 March of that year he rode in the Cheltenham Grand Annual Steeplechase at Withington; he and his horse *Zeno* were judged to have finished in a dead heat with Tom Oliver on *Greyling* and the riding prowess of the man was recognized. In subsequent years William Holman rode another four winners in the Grand Annual Steeplechase: *Dragsman* in 1842, when the race was held between Andoversford and Puesdown, *The Page* in 1843, again at Andoversford, *Stanmore* in 1847, at Noverton in Prestbury, and finally in 1852 on *Sir Peter Laurie* at Prestbury Park. *Sir Peter Laurie* was owned by Capt. William Barnett, the proprietor of Cleeve Lodge on Cleeve Hill.

William Holman, based in Prestbury, then concentrated on training horses. He trained three Grand National winners: *Freetrader* in 1856, *Little Charlie* in 1858 and *Anatis* in 1860. During the 1860s William Holman bought Cleeve Lodge and the stables from Capt. Barnett.

As the Holman family matured, five of the six sons developed a keen interest in horse racing. William Holman junior became the secretary and clerk of Cheltenham Racecourse in 1866 when the course was in Bouncer's Lane, Prestbury. The second son, George, equalled his father's record of five wins in the Cheltenham Grand Annual Steeplechase and also won three Prince of Wales Steeplechases. George, John and Alfred all rode in the Grand National, although none of them won. Alfred, the fourth son, after a career as a jockey and trainer, became clerk of the course at Prestbury Park and helped to lay out the present course. Along with F.H. Cathcart, Alfred instituted the first National Hunt Meeting at Cheltenham and is commemorated by the Holman Cup, a race held each year during April.

The youngest son, Frederick, rode for Stanhope Inglis, who lived at Lake House in Lake Street, Prestbury, a house that would have great relevance in future generations. Later he owned his own stud farm across the Evesham Road from Prestbury Park, where at one time he had a stallion named *Petronel* for whose services he charged 2 guineas, an extortionate sum at the time.

It is particularly through Frederick that the racing dynasty progressed. His son, William Frederick, a major in the army, was a good polo player and also a horse dealer. William's wife, Lucy, helped to nurse the troops treated at the Racecourse during the First World War. William had two children, a son, also named William, who rode in the 1955 Grand National, and a daughter, Diana, who much to the consternation of her mother married a jockey named Herbert D. Nicholson, who was more commonly known in the racing world as 'Frenchie'. After a very successful riding career, which included riding *Victor Norman* to victory in the 1936 Champion Hurdle, winning the Gold Cup in 1942 on *Medoc II* and being joint Champion Jockey in 1944–45 with Fred Rimell, he became a great trainer. Perhaps his greatest accomplishment was being able to bring on great jockeys. Among those who apprenticed with him were Pat Eddery, Walter Swinburn and Paul Cook.

To enhance this impressive racing lineage further, Frenchie's sister, Bobby, married the famous trainer, Willie Stephenson, who trained *Sir Ken*, the three-time Champion Hurdle winner.

Champion Trainer in successive seasons (1993–94 and 1994–95), David 'The Duke' Nicholson is the son of Frenchie and Diana Nicholson. After a riding career of almost 600 winners he has become in latter years one of the best trainers in the country, winning the 1988 Gold Cup with *Charter Party*. Highly rated by his peers (he advised and helped Princess Anne in her career as a race jockey), he works from perhaps the most modern training stables in the country, Jackdaws Castle, at Temple Guiting in Gloucestershire. In 1996–97 David Nicholson finished second in the trainers' championship but had 100 wins in the season and broke the £1 million barrier for prize money won.

The most remarkable and inspiring fact about David Nicholson is that throughout his life he has had to struggle against asthma and eczema caused by allergies to thirty-two different things, one of which is horses. His illness has often been very debilitating, limiting what he was able to do as a boy growing up. Yet he competed in all sports with a passion, both at school and later in adulthood, and refused to let the disability prevent him from becoming a figurehead in racing. To put this feat into perspective, the asthma attacks were often so bad he could not bend down to tie his shoe-laces and he was so allergic to horses that he could not saddle them or tack them up. Nevertheless he was and is a very determined person and so passionate about horses that his father had to carry him to the saddle so that he could ride. Apparently once he had mounted the asthma would leave him and he could relax.

In many ways David Nicholson is as much an inspiration to Cheltenham and to racing today as his great-great-grandfather, William Holman, was in the eighteenth century.

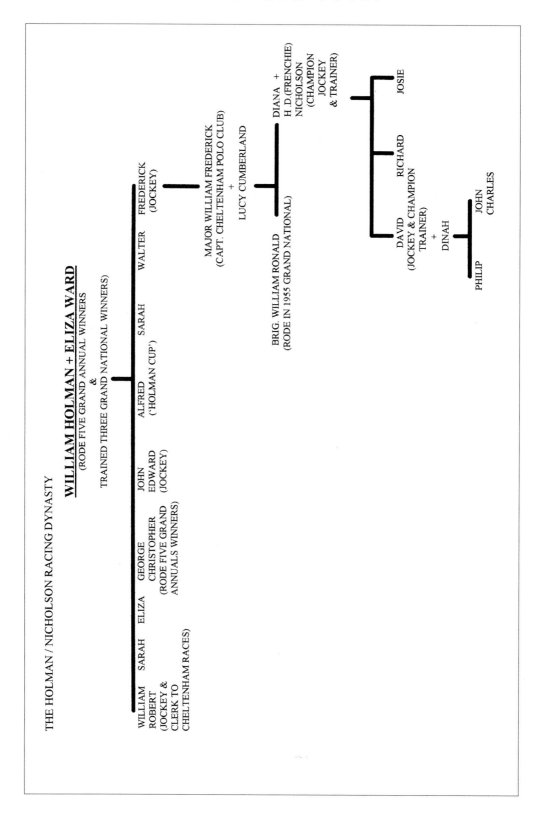

THE HOLMAN / NICHOLSON RACING DYNASTY

WILLIAM HOLMAN + ELIZA WARD
(RODE FIVE GRAND ANNUAL WINNERS)
&
TRAINED THREE GRAND NATIONAL WINNERS)

WILLIAM ROBERT (JOCKEY & CLERK TO CHELTENHAM RACES)

SARAH

ELIZA

GEORGE CHRISTOPHER (RODE FIVE GRAND ANNUALS WINNERS)

JOHN EDWARD (JOCKEY)

ALFRED ('HOLMAN CUP')

SARAH

WALTER

FREDERICK (JOCKEY)

MAJOR WILLIAM FREDERICK (CAPT. CHELTENHAM POLO CLUB)
+
LUCY CUMBERLAND

DIANA +
H. D. (FRENCHIE) NICHOLSON (CHAMPION JOCKEY & TRAINER)

BRIG. WILLIAM RONALD (RODE IN 1955 GRAND NATIONAL)

DAVID (JOCKEY & CHAMPION TRAINER)
+
DINAH

RICHARD

JOSIE

PHILIP

JOHN CHARLES

Cleeve Lodge on Cleeve Hill, the home of William Holman senior and his family during the 1860s, up to his death in 1888. The house was built with its stables in a disused quarry on Cleeve Hill in about 1850 by racing enthusiast Capt. Barnett for whom William Holman rode and later trained horses. Having moved from London, the Holman family resided at numerous locations in Cheltenham, including 2 Northfield Terrace, 3 Promenade Villas, Wellington Mews and St George's Mews. As he became more successful as a jockey and trainer, William was able to drop his shoemaking business and before moving to Cleeve Lodge he owned a farm – The Paddocks in Swindon Lane.

Cleeve Lodge is still a racing stables. Charlie Piggott (great-uncle to Lester) trained the 1939 Champion Hurdle winner, *African Sister*, from there, Bill Marshall continued the tradition and from 1969 Owen O'Neill has been in residence.

William Robert Holman (left) and brother
Alfred Holman photographed in the 1860s
when both were riding winners as amateur
jockeys. They were both instrumental in the
early days of Cheltenham Races. It is Alfred
who is commemorated with the Holman Cup
run every April at Cheltenham.

Alfred Holman (standing, centre) with invited members of the press and other officials of the Racecourse
after enjoying a lunch together, March 1911. F.H. Cathcart, with whom Alfred Holman designed and
built the Racecourse, is sitting in the middle of the front row; at this time he was the clerk of the course.

Tom Hobbs on his horse *Wood Pigeon*, June 1924. Tom Hobbs was an apprentice to John Holman in the 1860s. The Hobbs family retained a racing heritage over the years. Bruce Hobbs rode *Battleship* to win the 1938 Grand National, a horse trained by his father Reg. Bruce Hobbs is the godfather to David Nicholson and until the 1995 Festival, when David Nicholson's horses, *Kadi*, *Viking Flagship* and *Putty Road* gave him a treble in one Festival Day, Reg Hobbs had been the only trainer to accomplish the feat, back in 1942 on Gold Cup Day. Coincidentally, two of those rides in 1942 were by Frenchie Nicholson – *Medoc II* in the Gold Cup and *Jack Pugh* in the Spa Handicap Steeplechase.

Cheltenham Polo Club at Prestbury Park, 1930s. Captain of the Polo Club was William Frederick Holman whose daughter was to marry Frenchie Nicholson. William built up a pony stud at Lake House in Prestbury where he lived.

The West of England team playing the Maharajah of Jaipur's polo team which was touring England in 1933. The game was played at the Cheltenham Polo Club in the middle of Prestbury Park and Maj. William F. Holman played an important part in organizing the event. His wife should have acted as hostess, but as she was ill at the time their sixteen-year-old daughter, Diana, was left to carry out the role.

Crowds on both sides of the Racecourse strain to watch the finishing straight of the Newent Handicap Steeplechase, 14 March 1942. The 2-mile race, with a winner's purse of £300, was won by Herbert Charles Denton ('Frenchie') Nicholson who trained and rode *Matador* in a year when the Festival was run over two days, on successive Saturdays. On that same day *Forestation* won the Champion Hurdle.

The following week, 21 March, Frenchie Nicholson rode his Gold Cup victory. The 14 March meet was very much treated as a dress rehearsal for the Gold Cup; several of the leading horses lined up in the Grand Annual Steeplechase which was won by *Red Rower* from *Medoc II*, a reversal of the following week's result in the Gold Cup. Of particular interest is the number of men and women in uniform; this was the last festival to be staged during the war until March 1945.

Birthlaw, owned by Maj. W.R. Holman, jumps the hurdle nearest the camera on the way to winning the Rosehill Selling Hurdle Race on Saturday 6 January 1945. *Birthlaw* was ridden by Frenchie Nicholson in the first race held at Cheltenham for almost three years. This horse was later sold to Mrs V. Bruce for whom he continued his winning ways.

Saturday 10 November 1945 and the first race of the day kicks off another remarkable day for Frenchie Nicholson in a remarkable year. In February he had ridden four winners in a day at Cheltenham and then followed it up by winning three successive races the next day. At the end of the 1944–45 season he was crowned joint Champion Jockey with Fred Rimell, with fifteen wins each in a war-affected season. On this second day of the first meeting at Cheltenham in the 1945–46 season Frenchie rode another four winners and is the only jockey to have done so twice. This race, the Southam Novices' Steeplechase, was won by Nicholson on Mrs Carlos Clarke's *Karlstar*, seen here jumping the fence on the right.

Three fences from home, *Ethie Agnes*, ridden by L. McMorrow, leads the field in the Southam Novices' Steeplechase, 10 November 1945. The horse was subsequently disqualified and Frenchie Nicholson started his winning sequence. The two races of the day in which he didn't have a ride were the only ones he didn't win.

A waterjump for the Cheltenham Handicap Steeplechase, 10 November 1945. The race was won by Frenchie Nicholson on *Poet Prince*. The leader at this point is *Bestway*, ridden by C. Mitchell, who finished in fifth place, followed by *Cophetua* with E. Hannigan, who was pulled up, and then *Home Lover*, ridden by Don Butchers, who finished third.

The third race of the meeting, 10 November 1945. Frenchie Nicholson leads the Cheltenham Handicap Steeplechase on *Poet Prince* on his way to winning the race. The horse was owned by Mr D. Sherbrooke and was trained by Fulke Walwyn, who holds the Cheltenham record as the trainer with the most successes – 211. He trained all of Frenchie Nicholson's four wins on the day. *Poet Prince* was a previous Gold Cup winner in 1941, when he was ridden by Roger Burford and trained by Ivor Anthony. In second place to *Poet Prince* in the Cheltenham Handicap is *Master P*, ridden by Jack Molony.

The Dursley Handicap Hurdle Race, 10 November 1945. Frenchie Nicholson on Mr L. Milne's *Quartier Maitre* is leading Mrs V. Bruce's *Birthlaw* at the last flight. After winning this race Frenchie Nicholson went on to win the Pittville Handicap Steeplechase on *Kipper Kite* and thus complete a very successful day. Frenchie Nicholson rode a total of forty-eight winners at Prestbury Park.

Lake House in Lake Street, Prestbury, during the eighteenth century the home of Stanhope Inglis for whom William Holman's son, Frederick, rode. Frederick acquired the house himself in about 1893 and it remained in the family until after the Second World War. The stables attached to the house were used by Frenchie Nicholson for training before their eventual sale.

Frenchie Nicholson, the trainer. Operating from the stables at Lake House in Lake Street, Prestbury, Frenchie built up his reputation as a trainer, both of horses and young jockeys. He started training in 1946 when he and Diana were living at Sandford Dene in Lake Street and continued to train in the village until he retired at the end of 1979. Like most trainers in Prestbury, he took his horses up on to Cleeve Hill each morning for a good workout.

Frenchie Nicholson was a well-respected trainer and when Dorothy Paget moved her horses from Fulke Walwyn, it was to Frenchie that she entrusted them. Frenchie's legacy to the world of horse racing must surely be the way he brought the best out of aspiring apprentices, nurturing them into mature jockeys. He ran a very tight ship with his apprentices, worked them hard and was a great disciplinarian, but he was fair and took great pleasure in the successes of his boys. Some of the greatest names in flat racing came through his ranks (which is odd considering his propensity for jump racing), such as Walter Swinburn, Pat Eddery, Tony Murray and Paul Cook. His own son David, Michael Dickinson, Mouse Morris and Brough Scott became great jump jockeys under his tutelage.

Frenchie Nicholson died in Prestbury on 27 April 1984 at the age of seventy-four. The Frenchie Nicholson Conditional Jockeys' Handicap Hurdle Race held each autumn at Cheltenham reminds us all of the debt owed to him by the world of racing.

David Nicholson in his Oakley Hall school uniform at Cheltenham Races with his mother Diana, on the left, and P. Gilmour, on the right. Oakley Hall is a Cirencester school and David attended it from the age of seven. It was chosen by his parents because Cirencester is higher than Cheltenham and because the school was set on gravel – these features were believed to help David's chronic asthma.

David Nicholson winning his first hurdle race – not at Cheltenham, but at Chepstow – on *Fairval* on Easter Monday, 11 April 1955, at the age of sixteen. *Fairval*, as well as giving David his first hurdle race, gave his father, Frenchie, his last hurdle race – at Cheltenham in 1955 when they were unplaced.

Jackdaws Castle at Temple Guiting, the home and training stables run by David Nicholson. Owned by businessman Colin Smith (who also owned *Charter Party*, David Nicholson's 1988 Gold Cup winner), Jackdaws Castle is a purpose-built, state-of-the-art training establishment for racehorses, first opened in 1992. David Nicholson moved his training from his home at Condicote to work under contract for Colin Smith and in so doing leapt to the highest echelons of the trainers' ladder. His first season there brought 100 winners for the first time in his career, and in his second and third seasons he was Champion Trainer. In 1996–97 he trained 100 winners and topped £1 million in prize money. At present he has ninety-five horses in his care and two of the best young jump jockeys in the country, Robert Thornton (champion amateur National Hunt jockey, 1996–97), along with Robert Johnson, one of the country's top jockeys, and Adrian Maguire (twice Champion Jockey runner-up and Gold Cup winner on *Cool Ground* in 1992), who is his stable jockey. Like his father before him David Nicholson is a hard disciplinarian and taskmaster, and like his father he helps to produce great jockeys as well as great horses.

  In many ways Jackdaws Castle is the pinnacle and culmination of a dynasty reaching back over 175 years; the training facilities there are unique in Britain. Unfortunately, David Nicholson seems to be the end of the Holman/Nicholson racing line – neither of his sons seems likely to take up the reins.

NATIONAL HUNT
FINDS A HOME

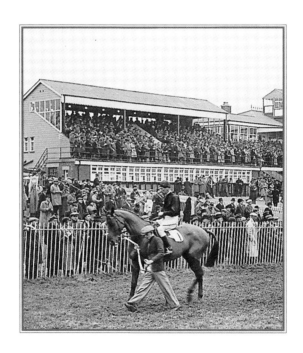

When W.A. Baring Bingham purchased Prestbury Park in 1881 for £25–30,000 he made it clear that he intended to bring racing back to the Park and that a racecourse would be mapped out. At first, however, he used the Park as a stud farm and it was not until 1898 that a race meeting was held there with a modicum of success. Four years later Prestbury Park held its first National Hunt Festival, 9–10 April 1902. It was the dream-child of F.H. Cathcart and Alfred Holman, who between them laid out the course and put all the plans together. The first race was the Cowley Maiden Chase which was won by *Both Ways*, a four-year-old bay gelding ridden by D. Davies and owned by T. Vale.

In 1894 Frederick Cathcart joined John Pratt of London in a business that Pratt had initially set up in 1860. They acted as inspectors for many the country's racetracks, supplying clerks to the courses, receiving entries, offering horse insurance and even acting as agent to trainers and jockeys.

In 1904 the National Hunt Steeplechase (inaugurated in 1860 at Market Harborough) was run at Cheltenham for the first time, with Ivor Anthony riding W.B. Partridge's *Timothy Titus* to victory. Two years later the course lost the race to Warwick, but in 1911 it returned to Cheltenham where it has remained ever since. For many years the National Hunt Steeplechase was the principal race held at Cheltenham and it took many years for first the Gold Cup and then the Champion Hurdle to overtake it in importance. It was not until after the First World War that prize money for these two races was more than that on offer for the National Hunt Steeplechase.

The Great Western Railway Co. opened a small station on its line on the north-eastern corner of the Park in 1906, specifically to cater for racegoers. The station had two 700 ft platforms and six years later installed a ticket office that had been made in prefabricated form at Swindon. This ticket office had three rooms, a booking office, booking hall and waiting room, and was wooden with a steel roof specifically designed to look like slate cladding – it is believed that this roof is the only example of this unusual design surviving today. Shelters and toilets were also added to the station and for many years the 'race day specials' would bring racegoers to the Racecourse by steam, playing an important part in linking the Racecourse to the rest of the country.

In 1908 the Cheltenham Steeplechase Co. was formed, with Frederick Cathcart, previously secretary of the Cheltenham Steeplechase Club, as its first chairman. The association between Pratt & Co. and Cheltenham Racecourse lasted until 1978; they were secretaries of the Steeplechase Company. In May 1908 the New Stand was opened for members of the club with a lawn in front on which teas were served. In 1911 the new course was complete and the impressive stands building programme was finally completed for the 1914 Festival.

The stands, however, were soon requisitioned. In October 1914 the Red Cross took them over for use as a troop hospital. The first patients were nursed in the ladies' drawing room, and subsequent ones were given the luncheon rooms. The jockeys' changing-room was used for patients' kit storage and the adjacent weighing room was used as an office. Evidence of their residency could be seen for many years in the Great Fireplace in the Tommy Atkins Bar where small indentations were visible, created by the soldiers 'chalking' up their billiard cues. Nevertheless, a few meetings survived the war. There was a Boxing Day Meeting in 1914 and a further six days of racing during the following year.

In 1919, with hostilities over, Ernest Robinson, who had joined Pratt & Co. in 1911, took over as clerk of the course and in 1923 the Festival Meeting was extended to three days, heralding an interwar period of sustained growth and interest in National Hunt racing. The Cheltenham Gold Cup was added to the Festival fixture list in 1924 and in 1927 the Champion Hurdle was born.

The interwar period also saw Prestbury Park used by the Cheltenham Polo Club which held frequent matches there and an occasional gymkhana. There were two boarded grounds mapped out in the middle of the Park with playing days being Tuesdays, Thursdays and Saturdays. They were meant to be the best grounds in the west of England; in May 1933 the Maharajah of Jaipur ('The Last Maharajah') brought a team over to England and, amid much publicity, played in Cheltenham.

These early Festival years at Cheltenham brought such great racing names as *Brown Jack*, *Insurance*, *Easter Hero*, *Golden Miller* and *Thomond II* to the track along with legendary owners like Miss Dorothy Paget, trainers such as Basil Briscoe and the Anthony brothers, Ivor and Jack, and jockeys, George Duller, Gerry Wilson, Fred Rimell, Billy Stott and 'Frenchie' Nicholson. They were almost halcyon days. Each Festival surpassed the last, but prize money still ranked well behind the Grand National meet at Aintree and far behind that offered in flat racing.

The weather inevitably caused some cancellations of meetings and races, but the greatest disruption came with the outbreak of the Second World War, when first the British and then the American troops requisitioned the Racecourse. From the end of the 1941–42 season (when *Medoc II* won the Gold Cup and *Forestation* the Champion Hurdle) until 6 January 1945 no racing was held at Cheltenham. However, a great tradition had been started and after the war Cheltenham Races and National Hunt racing would go from strength to strength. Cheltenham had become the home of the National Hunt and such it would remain.

The opening of the New Stand in May 1908, the same year that the Cheltenham Steeplechase Co. was formed. This was the first phase of an extensive building programme.

The Members' Lawn was opened with the New Stand in 1908 and it was here that Edwardian racegoers enjoyed teas and light refreshments.

The riders' numbers for the second race of the day, Festival Meeting, 1911.

The parade ring, March 1911. The horses of the next race are shown to the punters.

The completed stands on National Hunt Steeple Chase Day, 11 March 1914. The project had taken six years and was welcomed by record crowds for the Festival meet. Unfortunately it would be some years before it could really fulfil its potential. The First World War called upon its services as a Red Cross Hospital – a far cry from the designs that Cathcart, Holman *et al.* had had for it. Nevertheless, when racing returned to its pre-war stature the grandstand crowd swelled more and more each year. The impressive facilities at Cheltenham Races demanded attention from the racing world and it was soon heralded as an important venue for National Hunt racing. In effect it became, and has remained ever since,

the Home of the National Hunt and it was this great, innovative building programme that contributed so much to its reputation and status. During this century the grandstand has been improved and modernized, but the original building created a foundation for the fabulous grandstand that is there today. That first building programme fuelled the way for the future and it should be borne in mind when we consider the rise of Cheltenham Racecourse. It is not just about the Gold Cup and the Champion Hurdle; it is as much to do with the whole venue and the impression of grandeur that it conveys. (*photograph reproduced by kind permission of Cheltenham Art Gallery and Museum*)

Racegoers in the more expensive section of the course where they could preview the horses for the next race and consider the condition of each runner. Many of the women are wearing furs, all dressed up for the great occasion that the Cheltenham Festival was and remains. After being paraded around the ring, the horses were then led out on to the course and to their starting positions just as they are today.

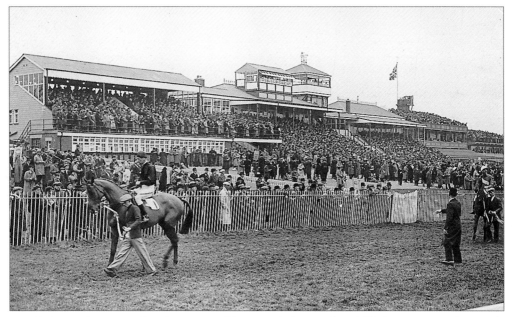

A packed Festival meeting after the First World War with the grandstand filled to capacity. The crowds watch the horses of the next race being led down from the parade ring to their starting positions.

The first fence in the National Hunt Steeplechase of 1926, which was won by *Cloringo*, a 25–1 outsider, ridden by W. Dutton, owned by J.C. Paterson and trained by Barthropp. Of the thirty-nine runners two fell at this first fence, *What's That* and *Old Bill*.

T. Griffiths falling from *St Caradoc* at the second fence of the National Hunt Steeplechase, 1926.

The last fence of the 1926 National Hunt Steeplechase, Wednesday 10 March. The leading horse, *Lissett III*, which was owned by Lord Grimthorpe and ridden by S. Dennis, was beaten in the run in by *Cloringo* who is jumping second. Finishing in third place was *Seti the First*.

The United Hunts Challenge Cup at the 1926 Festival. The leading horse is *Upper Grange* ridden by J. Norris who went on to take the race. *Upper Grange* was owned and trained by E.G. Pease. Jumping in second place is *Blank Cartridge*, ridden by Maj. Cavanagh, and third placed in the race was R. Gaskell on *Penguin*.

The four-year-old *Grakle*, ridden by E. Foster, in the 1926 Juvenile Steeplechase, with *Gun Runner*, ridden by W. Gurney, behind. Finishing in third was T. Gurney on *Irina*. Five years later, ridden by R. Lyall and trained by T. Coulthwaite, *Grakle* won the Grand National. The National ride was due to go to Tim Hamey, but he lost it after *Grakle* threw him and he had to have hospital treatment for a head wound – the owner thought that Hamey would not be fit in time and employed Coulthwaite. *Grakle* was a notoriously wayward horse and he gives his name to the cross noseband that was designed especially to control him.

A Festival meeting in the early 1930s. The racegoers' eyes are fixed on the race that unfolds in front of them. They are standing in the original Tattersall's Grandstand, named after the eighteenth-century horseman, Richard Tattersall, who was the first to organize bloodstock sales at Hyde Park Corner in London in 1766.

The first hurdle of the Lansdown Selling Handicap Hurdle Race held on the Wednesday of the three-day Festival meeting, 1933. First past the post was Keith Piggott on C.S. Green's *Togaro*, second was *Lord Puttenden* ridden by J. Millar and Tim Hamey finished in third on the odds-on favourite *Byron*.

The Maharajah of Jaipur's ponies and team entering the polo ground at Prestbury Park during their tour of England, May 1933. At Cheltenham they played the West of England polo team captained by Pat Roark.

The Maharajah, Sawai Man Singh II, selecting a polo stick. As well as the thirty-nine horses and fifty-one syces that the Maharajah brought to England he also brought his own polo stick maker. He is commonly referred to as 'The Last Maharajah' and is very much an icon of another epoch. Fabulously wealthy, he indulged his hobby of polo playing all over the world.

Members of the Maharajah's polo team. From left to right: Raj. Prithi Singh, Hamet Singh, Maharajah of Jaipur and Raj. Abbey Singh. Before coming to Cheltenham the Indians spent a month at Westonbirt to allow their ponies time to get used to the restricting boards used around polo grounds in England but not in India.

The crowds and entourage of the various teams watching the polo on Monday 22 May 1933.

Members of the West of England polo team. From left to right: Sir Ian Walker, Capt. J. Bailey, Pat Roark (captain) and D. J. Barton.

The game in action, which the Indians won, eleven goals to four.

The last fence of the 1936 National Hunt Steeplechase, with Herefordshire jockey E.W.W. Bailey on his way to winning on *Pucka Belle*. Second to finish was L. Elwell on *Duan Mor* and J. Rutter on *Kendal Kid* was third.

The third fence of the Newent Handicap Steeplechase, 8 March 1938. F.J. Honour's *Lateeve* with P. Lay is leading from *Corn Law*, ridden by E. Young, and *Running Sand*, jockeyed by R. Edgeley. *Lateeve* went on to win the race by 1½ lengths from *Corn Law* with *Running Sand* a further 3 lengths behind.

The Winners' Enclosure, 1930s.

A pre-war Champion Jockey's dinner. This is possibly the dinner held for Champion Jockey Gerald Wilson at the Plough Hotel, 15 November 1933. He was crowned Champion Jockey for the first time in the 1932–33 season; he then went on to be Champion six years in succession and seven in total. The dinner was laid on by the directors of the Steeplechase Co. (Cheltenham).

The Broadway Novices' Steeplechase two fences from home in the National Hunt meeting, Wednesday 13 March 1940. Leading is *Agleam*, ridden by T.F. Carey, the grey behind is *Vitement*, with D. Butchers, and right of him is *Sir Bill*, ridden by E.W.W. Bailey. Jumping on the far left is *Home Lover*, ridden by R. Morgan. The race was won by Lord Sefton's *Iceberg II*, ridden by Frenchie Nicholson, with *Sir Bill* in second and *National Night* in third.

The last National Hunt Meeting until 1945, the Seven Springs Handicap Steeplechase, 21 March 1942. *Home Lover* on the left, ridden by G. Archibald, trained by R. Hobbs and owned by L. Freedman, won the race. M. Jones on *The Hack*, jumping with him here, finished in third place. Gerald Wilson took the second place on *Marquery*.

THE CHELTENHAM GOLD CUP

The sport of steeplechasing evolved from hunting, with the first races being set over open countryside between the steeples of churches – hence the terms, steeplechasing and, in the less formal, amateur side of the sport, point-to-pointing.

On Wednesday 12 March 1924 the first Cheltenham Gold Cup, 3¼ miles over fences, was held for horses aged five years and upwards. The prize for the winner was a gold cup valued at 200 sovereigns and £685. Considering that the winner of the National Hunt Steeplechase held at the same Festival received £1,285, this was quite a modest prize.

The winner of that first Gold Cup was *Red Splash*, ridden by Dick Rees, trained by F.E. Withington and owned by Maj. H. Wyndham. The following year the winner received £880, but the prize money did not increase substantially over the next twenty years. Only once, in 1939, was more than £1,000 on offer, when *Brendan's Cottage* picked up £1,120. This was a brief pinnacle for the race. The war brought the prize money down to £495 and, at its nadir, £340 for *Red Rower* in 1945. From this point the prize money took off and in 1997 over £100,000 was waiting for Michael and Gerry Worcester when Tony McCoy brought their horse, *Mr Mulligan*, first past the winning post.

Dick Rees followed up his 1924 success on *Red Splash* with a win in 1928 on *Patron Saint*. The following year he won again, this time on *Easter Hero* and made it a Festival to remember by taking the Champion Hurdle on *Royal Falcon*. *Easter Hero*, became the first horse to win the race twice, racing to victory again in 1930, this time ridden by T. Cullinan.

In over seventy years of racing the Gold Cup has been cancelled in only four seasons. In 1931 frost made the going too hard and treacherous, snow caused the 1937 race to be abandoned and the Second World War prevented the running of the 1943 and 1944 races.

Every Gold Cup has brought its share of heroes, but some names stand out above the rest. Dorothy Paget's fabulous *Golden Miller* is one such name, winning the race for a record five successive years from 1932 to 1936. In 1934 he became the only horse to win the Grand National and Gold Cup in the same year. The 1932 win also gave Ted Leader a famous double, having won the Champion Hurdle riding *Insurance*, while in 1933 the same honours, with the same two horses, went to Billy Stott as jockey. When *Golden Miller* won in 1935, it was Gerry Wilson riding him and *Lion Courage* gave Wilson the Champion Hurdle winning ride that year.

Aubrey Brabazon rode *Cottage Rake* to victory during the Festivals of 1948–50 and ensured trainer Vincent O'Brien legendary status before he gave up training jump horses to concentrate on flat racing in 1959. In two of those years, 1949 and 1950, Aubrey Brabazon also did the 'double' when he rode *Hatton's Grace* in the Champion Hurdle.

Cheltenham's most successful horse, *Silver Fame*, won the cup in 1951, ridden by Martin Molony and trained by G. Beeby. *Silver Fame* won a total of ten races at Cheltenham, four of them coming in the 1949–50 season.

Tim Molony jockeyed a double in 1953, *Sir Ken* in the Hurdle and Vincent O'Brien's *Knock Hard* in the Gold Cup. The 1954 cup was won by the only horse to be trained locally, *Four Ten*, who came from John Roberts' Prestbury Court stables and was ridden by T. Cusack.

The last horse to win the cup in three successive seasons (1964–66) was the incredible *Arkle*, ridden by Pat Taaffe and trained by Tom Dreaper. Owned throughout his racing career by Anne, Duchess of Westminster, *Arkle* captured the romance and excitement that characterize Cheltenham and the Gold Cup.

L'Escargot won the cup in successive years (1970 and 1971), each time being ridden by T. Carberry, and is the last horse to have won the race more than once. T. Carberry won a third Gold Cup in 1975 with the Jim Dreaper-trained *Ten Up* and in 1980 he brought *Tied Cottage* first past the winning post after a superbly timed race, beating second-placed *Master Smudge* by 8 lengths, only for the horse to be disqualified after a routine dope test proved positive for theobromide – the first and only time that a Gold Cup winning horse has been disqualified. It was later proven that the drug had been accidentally ingested by the horse when he ate some contaminated feed and none of the horse's connections was ever under any suspicion of wrongdoing. It was a tragic way for the horse to lose the race, particularly after he had been runner-up to *Davy Lad* three years earlier.

Little Owl in 1981 gave Cheltenham a local winner as he was co-owned and ridden by Charlton Kings-based Jim Wilson, one of the best amateur riders of his day. Jenny Pitman became the first lady trainer of a Gold Cup winner in 1984 when *Burrough Hill Lad* won the honours, and seven years later she repeated the success with *Garrison Savannah*, another horse with local connections, this one owned by Cheltenham company, Autofour Engineering.

The 1983 Cup was an amazing and historic race for trainer Michael Dickinson who saddled the first five horses past the post, and one of the best postwar races must be that of 1991 with a field crammed full of past winners, Grand National winners and horses that would go on to win in future years.

Of all these great horses it is the winner of the 1989 Gold Cup that is perhaps regarded with the greatest of affection, not just by race fans but also by the general public. *Desert Orchid* focused more attention on Cheltenham and the Gold Cup than any other horse since *Arkle*. In many ways he has become the romance, the excitement and the courage that embodies this great steeplechase, now the 'blue riband' of National Hunt racing. It is the focal point of the Cheltenham Festival and very much the jewel in the crown for the Racecourse.

The first Cheltenham Gold Cup of 1924, won by *Red Splash*, ridden by Dick Rees. *Conjuror II* was second, with *Gerald L* coming up in third place. The cup itself was supplied by the jewellers, Martin & Co., of The Promenade in Cheltenham. When this cup went to auction on 29 March 1979 it fetched £2,600.

Martin and Co., the jewellers in The Promenade, Cheltenham. Martin's have held the permanent contract to supply the Gold Cup to Cheltenham, along with other trophies, since 1933, but previously supplied the very first Cheltenham Gold Cup of 1823 which was a 3-mile *flat* race won by Mr West's *Angelica*. Today's Gold Cup is made of 9 carat gold on a green onyx base and the design was chosen in 1972 by Brian Robinson, the then chairman of racecourse managers.

The first fence of the 1926 Gold Cup which was won by Tim Hamey on *Koko*, an unfancied 10–1 shot in a field of just eight horses. The winning prize money was £880, the highest it would be until 1939.

The last fence of *Koko*'s 1926 Gold Cup triumph, with *Old Tay Bridge*, ridden by J. Hogan, in second place and W. Filmer Sankey on *Ruddyglow* in third.

Tim Hamey and *Koko*, the horse he rode to victory in the Gold Cup of 1926. *Koko* was owned by Frank Barbour and trained by A. Bickley. At the time of the race he was an eight-year-old bay gelding, four years younger than the more fancied *Old Tay Bridge* who finished second. In 1932 Tim Hamey won the other great steeplechase, the Grand National, on *Forbra*. Born in Grantham, Tim Hamey moved to Bishops Cleeve, Cheltenham when he was eighteen and lived in the area for the rest of his life. After a successful riding career he became a well-respected trainer.

The great five-time Champion Jockey, in consecutive seasons from 1927/28–1931/32, Billy Stott (next-door neighbour to Tim Hamey on the Bishops Cleeve–Cheltenham road). He rode *Golden Miller* to the horse's second Gold Cup victory in 1933, beating *Thomond II* ridden by Stott's friend and other Bishops Cleeve neighbour, Billy Speck. In the same year Stott partnered Dorothy Paget's other great horse, *Insurance,* to victory in the Champion Hurdle, making him only the third jockey at that time to win both races during the same Festival. Despite his success, Dorothy Paget and her trainer Basil Briscoe overlooked Stott when they entered *Golden Miller* for the Grand National of 1933 and used Ted Leader instead.

Golden Miller, with Gerry Wilson, leading the way in the horse's penultimate Gold Cup victory. On the far side is Billy Speck on *Thomond II*, and jumping in third place is *Kellsboro Jack*, ridden by D. Morgan. These were the eventual finishing positions, the first two placings being identical to the great race of 1933 when Billy Stott was on the winner.

Forever surveying the parade ring at Cheltenham is this fabulous bronze statue of *Golden Miller*, the record five-time winner of the Gold Cup. Despite his incredible success it is interesting to note that these five wins brought Dorothy Paget a total of only £3,350 in prize money, and the total prize money over his career was £15,005. His career has few parallels – of his fifty-five races he won twenty-nine and was placed in thirteen.

The last fence of the epic 1935 race with *Golden Miller* (nearer the camera) and *Thomond II* almost neck and neck. *Thomond II* was a great horse, trained by Jock Whitney and just unfortunate to live in the same era as *Golden Miller*. Not only did he have two seconds to *Golden Miller* in the Gold Cup, but he finished in third place behind him when *Golden Miller* won the 1934 Grand National – the only horse ever to win the National and the Gold Cup in the same season. *Golden Miller* is still honoured today at Cheltenham with the running of the Golden Miller Handicap Steeplechase every spring. Billy Speck, *Thomond II*'s jockey in the race pictured here, was tragically killed the following month at the Cheltenham April meeting when he fell from his horse.

Cheltenham's most successful owner, the Hon. Dorothy Paget who, in her career as an owner between 1930 and 1957, had sixty-eight winners at Cheltenham, of which seven were Gold Cup winners and four Champion Hurdlers. Five of those Gold Cups came in successive years from 1932 to 1936 when *Golden Miller* dominated the race. *Roman Hackle*, ridden by Evan Williams and trained by Owen Anthony, made it six in 1940, and *Mont Tremblant*, ridden by D.V. Dick and trained by Cheltenham's most successful trainer, Fulke Walwyn, gave her her seventh.

Dorothy Paget was born in 1905, the second of Lord Queensborough's five daughters. She inherited a fortune, never married and became devoted to her horses and her gambling. The sums she ventured on races became legendary. She fell out with several of her trainers and eventually moved her horses to Frenchie Nicholson's stables in Prestbury, to whom she was loyal until her death in 1959, aged just fifty-four. Despite Dorothy Paget's reputation of being 'difficult', Frenchie Nicholson's widow, Diana, remembers her great generosity; she never forgot the birthdays of her jockeys and bought expensive Christmas presents. Her last Cheltenham winner was *Pelopidas*, ridden by D.V. Dick, who won the Churchdown Handicap Steeplechase on 16 October 1957.

Morse Code and Danny Morgan who beat *Golden Miller*, ridden by Frenchie Nicholson, in the 1938 race. Trained by Ivor Anthony and owned in partnership by Lt-Col. D.C. Part and Capt. J.W. Bridges, *Morse Code* was a previous winner of the Cheltenham Grand Annual Steeplechase and was the only horse ever to beat *Golden Miller* at Cheltenham.

Jumping on the left and blinkered is *Medoc II* with Frenchie Nicholson, well placed to make the move to win the 1942 race when the two horses that were well out in front, *Broken Promise* and *Solarium*, both fell at the last open ditch. *Red Rower* finished in second, reversing the previous week's result in the Grand Annual Steeplechase in a year when the Festival was held over successive Saturdays. In 1945 *Red Rower* finally took the Cup with D.L. Jones.

Arkle – possibly the greatest ever steeplechaser – stands proud at the Racecourse where he had some of his most famous victories. This bronze is by Doris Lindner. Born in 1957, trained by Tom Dreaper, owned by Anne, Duchess of Westminster and ridden by Pat Taaffe, *Arkle* would have totally dominated National Hunt racing in the mid-1960s but for the presence of the mighty *Mill House*, who took the Cup in 1963. The Gold Cups of 1964 and 1965 were his when he beat *Mill House* by 5 lengths and 20 lengths respectively and he made it three in a row when he beat *Dormant* by 30 lengths in 1966. He also won the Hennessy Gold Cup in 1964 and 1965, the Irish National in 1964, the Whitbread Gold Cup in 1965 and the King George VI Chase in 1965 – in fact of his twenty-six steeplechases he only failed to win four of them. He was so superior to his peers that the Irish rules of handicapping had to be changed in order to cater for him. In 1969 Cheltenham honoured *Arkle* by introducing the Arkle Challenge Chase, a 2-mile race run over the old course for five-year-olds and over. *Arkle* died at the age of thirteen on 31 May 1970 at Bryanstown in Ireland.

The Fred Rimell-trained *Royal Frolic*, winner of the 1976 Cheltenham Gold Cup, ridden by J. Burke and owned by Sir Edward Hanmer who received £18,134.50 in prize money. This was Fred Rimell's second victory as a trainer, having first won in 1967 with *Woodland Venture*, ridden by Terry Biddlecombe.

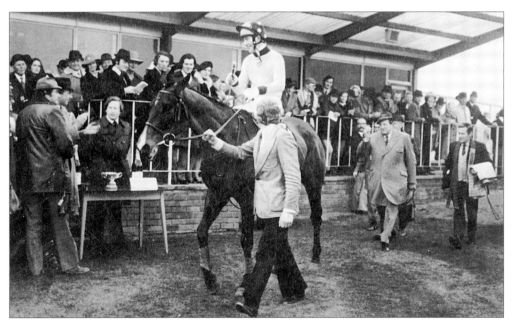

Royal Frolic after winning the 1976 Gold Cup. Fred Rimell brings up the rear. Second place in the race went to T. Carberry on *Brown Lad* and in third was F. Berry on *Colebridge*.

The second to last jump and Jim Wilson leads on *Little Owl* on his way to winning in 1981. Jim and his brother Robert had inherited *Little Owl* from an aunt, Bobby Grundy, at the start of the 1980–81 season. He was subsequently ridden by Jim in the colours of Robert. *Little Owl* was trained by Peter Easterby and beat off *Night Nurse*, the Champion Hurdle winner of 1976 and 1977, to win by just 1½ lengths. Jim Wilson, previously one of David Nicholson's amateur riders, was the first amateur to win the Gold Cup since 1947 when R. Black won on *Fortina*. He was an exceptional amateur jockey and between 1979 and 1982 he rode seven Festival winners, three of which were on *Willie Wumpkins* in the Coral Golden Hurdle for three consecutive years. With three winning rides in the 1980 Festival he was crowned Champion Festival Jockey and was the first recipient of the Ritz Club Charity Trophy.

Graham Bradley on *Bregawn* finishing second to Robert Earnshaw on *Silver Buck* in the 1982 Gold Cup. Both horses were from the training stables of Michael Dickinson, Champion Trainer 1981–82 to 1983–84. In 1983 Michael Dickinson improved his Gold Cup record with a feat never likely to be repeated, namely saddling the first five horses to finish the race. This time it was *Bregawn* that finished first, with Graham Bradley in the saddle, second was *Captain John* with David Goulding, third place went to *Wayward Lad* and Jonjo O'Neill, fourth was *Silver Buck* with Robert Earnshaw and fifth was *Ashley House* and Dermot Browne. After four dominant seasons in England Michael Dickinson moved his base to Maryland in the United States to train on the flat.

Desert Orchid leading the field on his way to winning the 1989 Gold Cup, ridden by Simon Sherwood. *Yahoo* with T. Morgan finished the race in second place and the previous year's winner, *Charter Party*, ridden by Peter Scudamore, was third. Simon Sherwood had already ridden *Desert Orchid* in eight races and had not been beaten on him. In the following two years' races *Desert Orchid*, ridden by Richard Dunwoody (who won a total of seven races on '*Dessie*'), finished in third place, behind *Norton's Coin* in 1990 and then *Garrison Savannah* in 1991.

Desert Orchid and *Yahoo* coming over the last fence. *Desert Orchid* was the first and, to date, only grey to win the coveted Gold Cup. He retired from racing in December 1991.

The 1990 Gold Cup first and second. The S.G. Griffiths-trained *Norton's Coin* (further from the camera), with Graham McCourt in the saddle, took the Cup from Mark Pitman on *Toby Tobias*.

Mark Pitman on *Garrison Savannah*, jumping with Graham McCourt on *Norton's Coin* in the 1991 Gold Cup. *Garrison Savannah* took the race, but *Norton's Coin* finished well out of it. After winning the Gold Cup Mark Pitman fractured his pelvis when he fell from his mount in the County Handicap Hurdle, the last race of Gold Cup Day. As a result he was unable to enjoy the evening's celebrations

The class-filled 1991 Gold Cup field, with, from left to right, *Party Politics*, ridden by A. Adams (1992 Grand National Winner), *Cool Ground*, with only jockey L. Harvey visible (1992 Gold Cup winner), *Desert Orchid*, with Richard Dunwoody (1989 Gold Cup winner), *Celtic Shot* and Peter Scudamore (1988 Champion Hurdle winner) and *Garrison Savannah*, ridden by Mark Pitman, just visible behind. *Garrison Savannah* went on to win the race and gave Jenny Pitman her second Gold Cup victory after P. Tuck won on *Burrough Hill Lad* in 1984. *The Fellow* (jockey Adam Kondrat) finished the race in second place (and won it in 1994) and *Desert Orchid* finished in third place.

Peter Scudamore on *Carvill's Hill* in the 1992 Gold Cup Race, eventually won by Adrian Maguire on *Cool Ground*. It was a controversial race in as much as *Carvill's Hill* started as the favourite and looked like being the horse to gain Peter Scudamore the prize he so coveted. However, from the start *Golden Freeze* led with *Carvill's Hill* and this close attendance possibly caused the favourite to make some bad mistakes. When *Golden Freeze* later pulled up having run himself out it was suggested that he had been in the race as a spoiler, but the Jockey Club later cleared trainer, Jenny Pitman, of all such accusations. *Carvill's Hill* led up to three jumps from home, but was then taken on and beaten out of the placings.

Gold Cup winner *Jodami*, ridden by Mark Dwyer, just trailing eventual second-placed *Rushing Wild* with Richard Dunwoody in 1993. *Royal Athlete*, ridden by Ben de Haan, finished in third and 1994 winners Adam Kondrat and *The Fellow* took fourth.

Norman Williamson on *Master Oats* on their way to victory in 1995. *Master Oats* was trained by Kim Bailey who in the same year trained the winner of the Champion Hurdle (*Alderbrook*, also ridden by Norman Williamson) and is only the third trainer to do the 'double' in the same year – Vincent O'Brien in both 1949 and 1950 and Peter Easterby in 1981.

THE CHAMPION HURDLE

T he sport of hurdle racing supposedly originated on the Brighton Downs when the Prince Regent and his entourage entertained themselves by racing over sheep hurdles. The first recorded hurdle race took place on Durdham Down, Bristol, 2 April 1821.

Three years after the Cheltenham Gold Cup was added to the National Hunt fixture list, the Champion Hurdle Challenge Cup was born. The year was 1927 and the National Hunt Festival was still very much in its infancy, but the race was acknowledged as an important step in Cheltenham's and National Hunt's future. £365 was on offer to the winner who turned out to be Mrs H. Hollins' *Blaris*, ridden by one of the all-time great hurdle-race jockeys, George Duller. It was an emphatic win which saw second-placed Billy Speck on *Boddam* trailing 8 lengths behind. Only *Insurance* in 1932 would win the race with such authority when he beat *Song of Essex* by 12 lengths.

Like the Gold Cup, the Champion Hurdle was brought into the Festival when Ernest Robinson was clerk of the course and illustrates what a significant part the man played in establishing Cheltenham's status as the home of National Hunt.

In 1928 the legendary *Brown Jack* won £680 for his owner, Sir Harold Wernher, *Royal Falcon* took the honours in 1929 and *Brown Tony* made it the first Gold Cup–Champion Hurdle double for his trainer, Jack Anthony, in 1930 (*Easter Hero* won the Gold Cup).

Like the Gold Cup, the Champion Hurdle was cancelled because of frost in 1931, and then 1932 saw the Hon. Dorothy Paget enjoy the first of her four Champion Hurdle victories when *Insurance* romped home. The following year he won again, becoming the first horse to win the race twice. With *Golden Miller* winning the Gold Cup in the same years, this was a double for both Dorothy Paget and her trainer, Basil Briscoe.

Another double for a trainer occurred in 1940, when *Solford* won the Hurdle and *Roman Hackle* the Steeplechase for Owen Anthony. The Vic Smyth-trained *Seneca* and *Forestation* were winners in 1941 and 1942 respectively, both horses being ridden by his nephew, Ron Smyth. After the wartime interruption, the second horse to win in successive seasons was *National Spirit*, also trained by Vic Smyth, in 1947 and 1948. This started a spate of multiple winners in the race.

Vincent O'Brien trained *Hatton's Grace* to win three years in succession from 1949 (in 1949 and 1950 he did the Gold Cup double with *Cottage Rake*), and then Willie Stephenson trained *Sir Ken* to repeat the record from 1952 to 1954. Tim Molony rode four winners in successive years when he partnered *Hatton's Grace* for the horse's last win and then *Sir Ken* for all of his victories, making him the most successful jockey in the Champion Hurdle Challenge Cup to date.

Cheltenham's most successful trainer, Fulke Walwyn (of the 211 races he won, 4 were Gold Cups, 2 were Champion Hurdles and 7 were Cathcart Challenge Cups), won both the Gold Cup (with *Mandarin*) and the Champion Hurdle(with *Anzio*) in 1962, and then *Kirriemuir* in 1965 brought him his second Champion Hurdle victory.

Fourteen years elapsed after *Sir Ken*'s last victory before a horse was found to win the race more than once. In 1968 *Persian War* won the first of three successive Champion Hurdles, ridden each time by Jimmy Uttley. His last victory ushered in a decade during which the status of the Champion Hurdle was consolidated. The 1970s was a decade of multiple winners and fantastic races. Fred Winter added to his victories as a jockey in 1955, 1959 and 1961 by training *Bula* to win the Champion Hurdle in 1971 and 1972 and *Lanzarote* in 1974. Fourteen years later he won again with Peter Scudamore on *Celtic Shot*. In 1973 and 1975 *Comedy of Errors* was first past the winning post, giving Fred Rimell the same distinction as Fred Winter and Gerry Wilson of both riding and training winners in the Champion Hurdle. Fred's widow, Mercy, continued the Kinnersley stables' success story by training *Gaye Brief* to win in 1983.

For six years three horses took a pair of victories each: *Night Nurse* (1976 and 1977), *Monksfield* (1978 and 1979) and *Sea Pigeon* (1980 and 1981). *Sea Pigeon*'s 1981 win gave his trainer Peter Easterby a Gold Cup–Champion Hurdle double for that Festival and a record five Champion Hurdle wins for a trainer. Apart from *Sea Pigeon*, the other victorious Easterby horses were *Night Nurse* and the 1967 winner, *Saucy Kit*. Jonjo O'Neill supplemented his 1980 victory on *Sea Pigeon* with a win on the much-loved *Dawn Run* in 1984, the first mare to win since *African Sister* in 1939. To date the last multiple winner is *See You Then*, who, trained by Nicky Henderson and ridden by Steve Smith-Eccles, won three Challenge Cups in successive years from 1985 to 1987.

The victories of *Celtic Shot* in 1988 and *Granville Again* in 1993 gave Peter Scudamore victories in a race that his father, Michael, never won, which must make up in some way for his failure to emulate his father's success in the Gold Cup. In 1989 and 1991 G.B. Balding trained *Beech Road* and *Morley Street* respectively to become champion hurdlers, while Martin Pipe added to his impressive record as a Champion Trainer with a victory for *Make A Stand* in 1997 to add to his win with *Granville Again* earlier in the decade.

Today the Champion Hurdle is one of the major races of the National Hunt calendar. Scheduled for the first day of the Cheltenham Festival it is second in importance only to the Cheltenham Gold Cup in those three vital days of racing. Winners of the Champion Hurdle are forever marked down in the record books. Winners of both great Cheltenham races are marked down as racing legends.

The first hurdle of the 1935 Champion Hurdle, with *Enchanter* leading the field and the blinkered *Hill Song* in second. Jumping in fifth place is the eventual winner, *Lion Courage*, ridden by Gerry Wilson and trained by F.A. Brown of Bourton-on-the-Hill. *Hill Song*, ridden by Belgian-born Georges Pellerin, finished in third place with Staff Ingham on *Gay Light* taking second.

Gerry Wilson was Champion Jockey six times and later, based in Andoversford, went on to train the 1945 Champion Hurdle winner, *Brains Trust*, ridden by Fred Rimell. Gerry Wilson was the first man both to ride and to train a Champion Hurdle winner. In 1973 Fred Rimell became the third man to do so when *Comedy of Errors* won the race for the first time. The great Fred Winter is of course the only other man to have accomplished this feat.

At Cheltenham, from left to right, Ted Walsh, Dr Michael Vincent O'Brien, Mrs Jacqueline O'Brien and Ivor Herbert. In an incredible period spanning from March 1948 until March 1959 Vincent O'Brien trained the winners of twenty-three Festival races, most notably four Gold Cups (*Cottage Rake* three times from 1948 to 1950 and *Knock Hard* in 1953), three Champion Hurdles (*Hatton's Grace*, 1949–51) and ten Supreme Novices' Hurdles. For eleven years he had at least one winner at the Festival and only his decision to turn to flat race training prevented him from winning more – in 1961 his former horse, *Saffron Tartan*, won the Gold Cup for his new trainer, Don Butchers. As a National Hunt trainer he was Champion Trainer twice, in 1952–53 and 1953–54, and to add to his Cheltenham honours he won the Grand National three times – 1953 with *Early Mist*, 1954 with *Royal Tan* and 1955 with *Quare Times*. When he turned to flat racing he flourished: he was Champion Trainer in 1966 and 1967 and trained the winners of thirteen Derbys (six English, six Irish and one French). Among his most famous horses on the flat are *Nijinsky* and *Sir Ivor*. He retired in October 1994 at the age of seventy-seven.

Standing on the left with friends are Fred Rimell and his wife, Mercy, at Cheltenham. Their success at Cheltenham as trainers is only bettered by Fulke Walwyn. Between them they trained 190 winners which included 2 Gold Cups, 3 Champion Hurdles and 4 Mackeson Gold Cups (the latter in consecutive years from 1968 to 1971, making him the only trainer to accomplish this feat). Fred saddled trebles at Cheltenham on four occasions – in 1950, 1968, 1970 and 1975.

During his riding career Fred Rimell was Champion Jockey four times and rode forty-two winners at Cheltenham between 1931 and 1946, including *Brains Trust* to win the 1945 Champion Hurdle, and four of them came all on one day, 31 March 1945.

He gave up riding after breaking his neck for the second time when he fell from his mount, *Coloured Schoolboy*, in the 1947 Gold Cup. Ten years later he trained the winner of the Grand National, *E.S.B.*, a feat he would achieve another three times with *Nicolaus Silver* in 1961, *Gay Trip* in 1970 and *Rag Trade* in 1976, the same year that his horse *Royal Frolic* won the Gold Cup.

Comedy of Errors with Ken White up, winning his second Champion Hurdle in 1975. The previous year he had been beaten by 3 lengths by the Fred Winter-trained *Lanzarote* and first won the Challenge Cup in 1973, as ridden by Bill Smith. A remarkable horse, owned by Ted Wheatley, *Comedy of Errors* won twenty-three of his forty-eight races, five of them at Cheltenham. He was trained throughout his career by Fred Rimell at his stables at Kinnersley in Worcestershire.

Sea Pigeon, the Champion Hurdle winner in 1980 and 1981. After finishing second to the great *Monksfield* in the 1978 and 1979 Champion Hurdle, *Sea Pigeon*, ridden by Jonjo O'Neill, finally took the 1980 Challenge Cup by 7 lengths from his great adversary. The following year, with John Francome in the saddle, he matched *Monksfield*'s achievement.

Gaye Brief in retirement at the age of twenty, still a striking and fit-looking horse. When Fred Rimell died suddenly in the summer of 1981, Mercy Rimell took over the training of the horses in their yard at Kinnersley. This was not unexpected as her whole life had revolved around horses in one way or another, whether it was showjumping or point-to-pointing. Furthermore, she had always been the one to determine which races were best suited for the horses that Fred trained.

In 1983 *Gaye Brief,* the last horse bought by Fred, won the Champion Hurdle for Mercy, with Richard Linley in the saddle. It was, like all the successes, a victory for both the Rimells; Mercy's determination and strength of character had nurtured the talent that Fred had first seen in the young horse.

Both *Gaye Brief* and Mercy Rimell now enjoy a well-earned retirement, both of them having given so much to racing and to Cheltenham.

The 1984 Champion Hurdle and 1986 Gold Cup winners, *Dawn Run* and Jonjo O'Neill, forever watching the Cheltenham parade ring. A legendary horse owned by Charmian Hill and trained by Paddy Mullins, she was the darling not just of her native Ireland but among all race fans. The first mare to win the Champion Hurdle since *African Sister* in 1939, she is the only horse ever to win both Cheltenham classic races. Her career was prematurely ended when she broke her neck in the French Champion Hurdle, just three months after having won the Gold Cup.

See You Then being paraded in Cheltenham before the 1987 Champion Hurdle. He was attempting to win the race for a third successive year, an achievement only previously accomplished by three horses: *Hatton's Grace*, *Sir Ken* and *Persian War*. Trained by Nicky Henderson, *See You Then* had beaten *Gaye Brief* into second place in 1986 when *Gaye Brief* was ridden by Peter Scudamore.

The first hurdle of the 1987 Champion Hurdle with Peter Scudamore leading the field on *Corporal Clinger*. Steve Smith-Eccles would eventually take the race for the third time on *See You Then* with *Flatterer* finishing second and *Barnbrook Again* in third.

Champion Jockey a record eight times (one title being shared with John Francome), Peter Scudamore
brings *Celtic Shot* past the winning post, 15 March 1988. *Celtic Shot* was trained by Fred Winter, the only
man to have won both the Gold Cup and Champion Hurdle as both a jockey and a trainer. This win was
Fred Winter's last Cheltenham victory. Peter Scudamore finished the following race season with a record
221 winners.

Kribensis, ridden by three-time Champion Jockey Richard Dunwoody, winning the 1990 Champion
Hurdle for trainer Michael Stoute. Richard Dunwoody is today the second most successful jockey over
jumps – only Peter Scudamore has ridden more winners. The owner of *Kribensis*, Sheikh Mohammed, had
another victor two years later when *Royal Gait* took the Cup, ridden by Graham McCourt.

Peter Scudamore's second Champion Hurdle success was on *Granville Again* in 1993. Second from the right in the Barbour jacket is Champion Trainer, Martin Pipe. When Peter Scudamore retired in April 1993 he had accumulated a National Hunt record of 1,678 winning rides, 792 of which were for Martin Pipe. He has also been Champion Jockey at the Cheltenham Festival on more occasions than any other jockey – three times in 1986, 1987 and 1991 – and has ridden a total of thirteen Festival winners.

Peter followed in the footsteps of his father, Michael, who had success in the Gold Cup when he rode *Linwell* for trainer C. Mallon in 1957, but never in the Champion Hurdle; by contrast Peter never won a Gold Cup. Peter Scudamore is now assistant trainer to Nigel Twiston-Davies at Naunton in the Cotswolds. (*photograph reproduced by kind permission of Bernard Parkin*)

The 1994 winners of the Champion Hurdle, Mark Dwyer with *Flakey Dove*. *Flakey Dove* was only the third mare to win the Champion Hurdle and the first since *Dawn Run* ten years previously. She was trained by Ryan Price and owned by Mr J.T. Price. Finishing in second was P. Holley on *Oh So Risky*, with Jamie Osborne taking third on *Large Action*.

The Champion Hurdle winner of 1996, six-year-old *Collier Bay*, ridden by Graham Bradley, the 1983 Gold Cup-winning jockey on *Bregawn*, and trained by Jim Old. *Alderbrook*, ridden by Richard Dunwoody, came second, but Jamie Osborne, who had been offered the ride on *Collier Bay*, fatefully took *Mysilv* instead and finished well down the field.

Champion Jockey Tony McCoy taking *Make A Stand* over the last hurdle on his way to winning the 1997 Champion Hurdle in a Festival year when he also saddled the Gold Cup winner, *Mr Mulligan*. He also rode *Or Royal* to victory in the Cathcart Challenge Cup Steeplechase during the Festival which, added to his second placings, allowed him to beat Richard Dunwoody to the position of Champion Festival Jockey. *Make A Stand* was the second victory in the race for trainer Martin Pipe, after Peter Scudamore's success of 1993, and one of four victories for him in the 1997 Festival.

SINCE THE WAR

On 6 January 1945 the first races for almost three years were held at Cheltenham. The first race, the Rosehill Selling Hurdle Race, was very much a local affair with Frenchie Nicholson winning on the Charlie Piggott-trained and Maj. Holman-owned *Birthlaw*, with Davy Jones on *Clarendon* coming second. The meetings for the rest of that 'season' were crammed full with races; in seven days of racing (the last being on 31 March) there were a total of fifty-five races, nine on one day in February and twenty-two being ridden during the three-day Festival.

However, as life returned to normal throughout the country, life returned to normal at Prestbury Park. The 1946 Festival saw the first great Irish invasion at Cheltenham where they won five of the Festival races, including the Gold Cup and the Champion Hurdle. The same year saw the Kim Muir Memorial Challenge Cup run for the first time, won by Capt. D. Baggallay on *Astrometer*. Kim Muir had been an amateur rider of talent who lived at Postlip Hall at the base of Cleeve Hill; he was killed in action at the age of just twenty-three. Today the Kim Muir Challenge Cup is still run during the Festival but it is now a co-memorial for Fulke Walwyn, the legendary trainer who saddled 211 winners at Cheltenham.

In 1948 Cheltenham was televised for the first time by the BBC newsreel; the Gold Cup was shown four days after it had been run. Fans would have to wait another six years before full coverage of the Festival with commentary by Peter O'Sullevan was broadcast.

For the first five years after the war the amateur Champion National Hunt jockey was Lord Anthony Mildmay of Flete who rode several winners at Cheltenham, mostly for trainer Peter Cazalet, including the 1950 Festival winner *Manicou* in the Broadway Novices' Steeplechase. Two months after that victory he drowned while bathing off the Devon coast. A landowner of some note, he was a steward as well as a jockey, and was respected by all in the sport. The following year the Mildmay of Flete Challenge Cup was introduced to the Cheltenham Festival and has been run ever since.

On 2 March 1954 Lester Piggott rode his one and only Festival winner when he took *Mull Sack* to victory in the Birdlip Selling Hurdle Race, a horse trained by his father, Keith. In November 1957 the first sponsored race was held at Cheltenham, the Hennessy Gold Cup, which was won by P. Madden on the Fulke Walwyn-trained *Mandarin*, owned by Madame K. Hennessy. This race was held for three successive years until, in 1960, it became the Mackeson Gold Cup which it remained until 1996 when it became the Murphy's Gold Cup, today regarded as the first classic of the National Hunt season. Originally run over 2 miles, an extra ½ mile was added in 1967.

The 2-mile Champion Chase was added to the Festival Meeting in 1959 and was renamed in 1980 to become the Queen Mother Champion Chase. Yet another Gold Cup was added to Cheltenham's fixture list in 1963, the Massey-Ferguson Gold Cup (now the Tripleprint Gold Cup) run over 2½ miles and in 1967 it was moved to the New Course for the first time. In 1988 both early season Gold Cups were won for the first time in the same season by one horse, *Pegwell Bay*, trained by Tim Forster.

In 1964 the races at Cheltenham were put under some pressure. There was concern that the land could be sold for building and Lord Wigg of the Levy Board was supposedly looking at moving the National Hunt Festival to Sandown. As a consequence the Racecourse Holdings Trust consortium was formed which bought the course for £240,000. Today this consortium owns twelve of the country's fifty-nine courses and, as it is a subsidiary of the Jockey Club, once expenses and wages have been paid, all profits are put back into the sport.

The Triumph Hurdle was brought to Cheltenham in 1965, having been inaugurated at Hurst Park in 1939 where it had been run every year until the park's closure. For two years, 1963 and 1964, the Triumph Hurdle was not run at all. Then, in April 1965, it was brought to a Cheltenham Meeting with *Blarney Beacon* being the first winner out of a field of just seven. The great *Persian War* won the race in 1967 and then in 1968 the Daily Express Triumph Hurdle moved to the Festival meeting where it has remained ever since.

The Racecourse station was closed on 25 March 1968, but then reopened on 18 March 1971 for the Festival and was even used by the Queen on 7 April of that year when she visited the course. It was finally closed after the 1976 Festival meeting.

In 1970 the first colour broadcast of the Cheltenham Festival hit television screens, and by the end of the decade a new building programme had been started to modernize the Racecourse in order to create not just more and better facilities for the ever-increasing crowds but also a better spectacle for the television visitor.

Mrs Jackie Brutton was the first lady trainer of a winner at Cheltenham when *Snowdra Queen* won the 1968 United Hunts Challenge Cup and ten years later the first winning lady jockey was Miss C. Saunders on *Ptarmigan* in the Vale of Evesham Hunters' Chase in May 1978. Miss C. Beasley was the first lady jockey to win a Festival race in 1983 when *Eliogarty* won the Christie's Foxhunter Challenge Cup and at the same Festival Mrs Mercy Rimell became the first lady trainer of a Champion Hurdle winner when *Gaye Brief* took the honours. The following year Mrs Jenny Pitman became the first lady trainer to take the Gold Cup.

In 1980 the first Ritz Club Charity Trophy was inaugurated for the jockey with the most winning rides during the Festival and was awarded to Jim Wilson. This trophy has subsequently become the London Clubs Charity Trophy.

The 1980s was a period of major growth for the Racecourse in the corporate entertainment business; this decade also saw the introduction of the tented village for the Festival meeting which adds over 10,000 per day to the capacity of the course. Channel Four took over the contract to televise Cheltenham racing in 1994, which ended a forty-year association with the BBC.

The 1995 Festival was a four-day event for the first time in its history because of a premature end to the Cheltenham season as a result of a flood relief scheme in Prestbury. The fourth day was not a part of the National Hunt meeting and to date there have been no indications that future Festivals will be extended to four days.

The Cowley Novices' Hurdle Race (Division II) on the second day of the new Cheltenham season, 10 November 1945. The race was won by G. Kelly on *Filum*, but the day would be remembered for Frenchie Nicholson's four winning rides.

Filum leading the field to go on to win the Cowley Novices' Hurdle Race (Division II), 10 November 1945. *Filum* was owned by D. Goulding and trained by C. Kelly. Second place went to Fred Rimell on *Meseta Moon*. Fred Rimell had an impressive two days at the Cheltenham meet, riding three winners and three seconds out of the twelve races. Third place in the above race went to Bill Denson on *Tacitus*.

The Cowley Novices' Hurdle Race (Division III), 10 November 1945. The last race of the day, it was won by the Gerry Wilson-trained *Carnival Boy*, ridden by Fred Rimell, with J. Cox on *Causeway* and T. Farmer on *Red Ribbon* coming second and third respectively.

The Leckhampton Novices' Steeplechase, 29 December 1950. The eventual winner, *Ordnance*, ridden by J. Humphreys and trained by Fred Rimell for Mrs W.J. Rimell, is leading the field from local jockey Rex Hamey on *Yonder Hill*. Only these two horses were to finish the race.

An early 1960s postcard of the new grandstand at Prestbury Park which was opened in 1960. The original stands of the first two decades of the century are still visible beyond it.

Jockey Bob Champion unsaddling a mount at Cheltenham. He is particularly known for his courageous fight against cancer and subsequent success in the 1981 Grand National on *Aldaniti*, an equally courageous horse who had fought back from a terrible accident to race again. In 1979 Bob Champion partnered *Aldaniti* to third place in the Gold Cup behind Jonjo O'Neill on *Alverton*. Of Bob Champion's four Gold Cup rides, this was his best placing.

Starting from the Royal Mews, Buckingham Palace on 1 March 1987, *Aldaniti* made a 250-mile sponsored walk, finishing at Aintree on 4 April. For each mile he had a different rider and each rider had to raise £1,000 in sponsorship which all went towards the Bob Champion Cancer Trust. Princess Anne was the jockey of *Aldaniti* when he arrived at Cheltenham Racecourse during the Festival meeting for that part of his walk.

The jockeys in the 1981 Kim Muir Memorial Challenge Cup show their mounts one of the fences that they will have to face. In the centre is Prince Charles, Prince of Wales on his own horse, *Good Prospect*. Unfortunately the horse and rider parted company at the tenth fence .In his short career as a steeplechase jockey, Prince Charles never rode a winner but he did finish second in a handicap chase at Ludlow in October 1980.

In 1985 Princess Anne took up race riding and, with guidance from David Nicholson, rode in several races, first on the flat where she had notable wins at Ascot, Newmarket and York, and later over jumps, her first victory being on the Josh Gifford horse, *Cnoc Na Cuille*, at Worcester in 1987. She rode two races at Cheltenham in April 1986. In the first one she came fourth on her own horse, *Wishing Well*, and in the second, the Amateur Riders' Association National Hunt Flat Race, she rode Mrs Jenny Mould's *Salmon Run* but was unplaced.

Seven-time Champion Jockey (six times outright, once jointly with Peter Scudamore in 1981–82) John Francome on *Cilium*, a horse owned by Lord Howard de Walden and trained by Fred Winter. He rode a total of 1,138 winners from 5,061 mounts between 1970 and 1985, 575 of which were for trainer Fred Winter. He won both the Gold Cup (1978 on *Midnight Court*) and the Champion Hurdle (1981 on *Sea Pigeon*) at Cheltenham as well as numerous other Festival and non-Festival races. In 1981 he was the Champion Jockey of the Cheltenham Festival when he had three winning rides. He is now a regular presenter of *Channel Four Racing* and is a respected novelist.

Seamus O'Neill being led on the French horse, *Fealty*, after winning the 1984 Sun Alliance Novices' Hurdle for trainer Peter Brookshaw, the nephew of Tim Brookshaw, at odds of 33–1. *Fealty* shattered the course record by over 3 seconds to win the race and beat *Bajan Sunshine*, ridden by Peter Scudamore, into second place and Steve Smith-Eccles on *Contester* into third.

Fourth from the left in the front runners is Richard Dunwoody on *Kribensis* on his way to winning the 1988 Daily Express Triumph Hurdle. *Wahiba* came second and the Martin Pipe-trained *Chatam* (who went on to win the 1991 Cathcart Challenge Cup) was third. *Kribensis* was trained by Michael Stoute and owned by Sheikh Mohammed; two years later he took the Champion Hurdle.

One of the unscheduled attractions of Gold Cup Day in 1988 was this late finisher, passing the winning post to the cheers and delight of the crowd.

Having picked up his clothes he makes a run for it, hotly pursued by a policewoman who unfortunately tripped over as she tried to keep herself focused on the mission.

He is eventually tackled before he can get to the fence – the police get their man!

The police encourage the gentleman to cover himself up and lead him off the course. He was later released without charge but encouraged to give a sizeable donation to charity.

Her Royal Highness, the Queen Mother arriving at Cheltenham. She is the sport's most loved patron and each year presents the trophy to the owners of the winning horse of the Queen Mother Champion Chase. The 2-mile Champion Chase was inaugurated in 1959 with *Quita Que* taking the first honours, ridden by J. Cox. In 1980 the Queen Mother graciously agreed for the Chase to be renamed in her honour. In that first Queen Mother Champion Chase there was some unfortunate controversy when the winning horse, *Chinrullah*, was disqualified on technical grounds and second to finish, *Another Dolly*, was installed as the winner. Although in its history several horses have won the race twice, only one horse has won it three times – *Badsworth Boy*, 1983–85.

One of the most popular horses to race in recent years, *Desert Orchid*, finishing the 1988 Queen Mother Champion Steeplechase in second place, ridden by Charlie Brown, to second-time winner, *Pearlyman*. Trained by David Elsworth, *Desert Orchid* won the Gold Cup the following year.

Barnbrook Again, ridden by Simon Sherwood, winning the Queen Mother Champion Chase on 15 March 1989 for the first of two consecutive wins. Trained by David Elsworth, *Barnbrook Again* won the race the following year, ridden by Hywel Davies, just beating the David Nicholson-trained *Waterloo Boy*, ridden by Richard Dunwoody. In that year both first- and second-placed jockeys were subsequently given a two-day ban for excessive use of the whip.

This atmospheric picture was taken by local photographer, Terry Bliss, and is of the exhausted field after the 1989 Ritz Club National Hunt Handicap Chase which was won by *Dixton House*, ridden by T. Morgan and trained by J. Edwards.

Miss Katie Rimell (now Johnston) in the saddle of *Three Counties* after her 1989 victory in the Foxhunter Challenge Cup. *Three Counties* was trained by Katie's grandmother, Mercy Rimell, at Kinnersley who retired in the same year having trained thirty-two Cheltenham winners since taking over from her husband, Fred. This race has been won by lady riders on three occasions: Caroline Beasley in 1983, Katie Rimell in 1989 and Polly Curling in 1996.

Trapper John, ridden by Charlie Swan, winning the Bonusprint Stayers' Hurdle, 13 March 1990. *Trapper John* was trained by M.F. (Mouse) Morris in Ireland and owned by Mrs P. Fanning. In the 1990 Festival this was the only winning ride for Charlie Swan, but in 1993 he rode four winners and in 1994 three winners, being the Champion Jockey of the Festival in both years and the first Irishman to win the Ritz Club Trophy.

The parade ring after the 1991 Queen Mother Champion Chase with the result on the board in the background. *Katabatic* won the race, with *Waterloo Boy* taking second and *Nos Na Gaoithe* third. *Katabatic* was ridden by Simon McNeill and trained by A. Turnell.

The Queen Mother presenting the trophy to Pell-mell Partners, the winning owners of *Katabatic* who had just seen off the David Nicholson-trained *Waterloo Boy*, ridden by Richard Dunwoody, to win the Queen Mother Champion Chase, 1991.

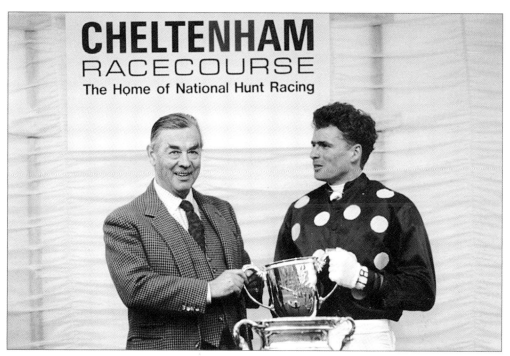

A presentation by the late Miles Gosling, former chairman of Cheltenham Racecourse and its parent company, Racecourse Holdings Trust. (*photograph reproduced by kind permission of Bernard Parkin*)

Richard Dunwoody riding *Flakey Dove* in the Cleeve Hurdle Race on the last Saturday, January 1994. In beating *Sweet Duke* by 6 lengths *Flakey Dove* gave Richard Dunwoody his 1,000th career win and made him only the fourth jump jockey to achieve this feat after Stan Mellor, Johnny Francome and Peter Scudamore. Richard Dunwoody was Champion Jockey for three successive years, 1992–95, and has won all three major National Hunt races, the Grand National, the Cheltenham Gold Cup and the Champion Hurdle. Ridden by Mark Dwyer, *Flakey Dove* won the 1994 Champion Hurdle.

The 1996 Bonusprint Stayers' Hurdle with *Cyborgo*, ridden by D. Bridgwater, beating the wonderful *Mysilv*, ridden by J.A. McCarthy. The Bonusprint Stayers' Hurdle was introduced in the 1972 Festival, replacing the Spa Hurdle which is now run at Cheltenham's New Year meeting.

Klairon Davis (left), ridden by F. Woods, on his way to beating Charlie Swan on *Viking Flagship* (centre) into second place and Richard Dunwoody on *Sound Man* (right) into third for the 1996 Queen Mother Champion Chase.

Lanfranco (Frankie) Dettori, one of the best flat race jockeys in the sport today if not ever, doing something he is unlikely to do with a horse – jump one of Cheltenham's famous hurdles. Frankie Dettori was the first teenager in 1990 to ride 100 winners in Britain since Lester Piggott in 1955. Born in Milan in December 1970 he moved to Newmarket to serve his apprenticeship and has not looked back since. On 28 September 1996 at Ascot he accomplished the incredible feat of becoming the first person to win all seven races on a race card.

The Queen Mother Champion Chase, 1997. From left to right: *Ask Tom*, ridden by R. Garritty, *Martha's Son* with R. Farrant and *Viking Flagship* with Richard Dunwoody. *Martha's Son*, trained by Tim Forster and owned by Paddy Hartigan and Michael Ward Thomas, won the race. Trained by David Nicholson, *Viking Flagship* won the chase two years in succession, ridden by Adrian Maguire in 1994 and in 1995 by Charlie Swan.

Richard Dunwoody on the Gordon Richards-trained *One Man*, winning the Pillar Chase for six-year-olds and over, Saturday 25 January 1997. This is the only race this great steeplechaser has won at Cheltenham. The David Nicholson-trained *Barton Bank*, ridden by Adrian Maguire, came second and Josh Gifford's *Yorkshire Gale* was third with Norman Williamson in the saddle.

THE EFFECT ON THE TOWN

When Cheltenham held its first race meetings the effect on the town was considerable. Balls and dinners were held, plays put on specially, and entertainments from out of town, such as an 'exhibition of wild beasts', were attracted by the large numbers of people congregating on Cleeve Hill and in Cheltenham. All manner of merchants set up stalls on the hill to sell their wares, and most boarding houses, inns and pubs found themselves full to the brim. The traffic congestion in Prestbury was of note as carriages attempted to make their way through the streets and up the poor road to the hill. By all accounts the first races of the early eighteenth century brought the same sort of consequences as they do today, albeit on a smaller scale. There was prosperity for some, inconvenience for others and, with the deluge of pickpockets and other riffraff, misery for some.

Today the Cheltenham Races are a part of the town throughout the year, although in Festival Week and for the Murphy's meeting their effect is much more noticeable. There are several pubs that honour the sport – the Horse and Jockey, the National Hunt, the Dawn Run and the Golden Miller to name just a few.

In the 1960s a whole estate was built in the Wymans Brook area of Cheltenham, just off Swindon Lane which leads directly to the racecourse, honouring past equine heroes of Cheltenham. Mandarin Way, Pendil Close, Cottage Rake Avenue, Roman Hackle Road and Seneca Way can all be found on the estate.

However, the most obvious effect that the Races have on the town comes in Festival Week when everyone prepares for the massive influx of racegoers. For one week the town gets totally transformed from a conservative, modern spa to a vibrant hive of activity. Most of the pubs run some sort of promotion for the week and for one week in the year live music can be heard everywhere – even the most stalwart of local rock 'n' rollers manage to fit a couple of Irish melodies into their repertoire.

Local shops are suddenly full of racing merchandise, bookshops are crammed full with form guides, yearbooks and anything else with a racing bent. Clothes shops display the latest racing fashions along with healthy selections of Barbours, caps and umbrellas. Picture shops suddenly have a fine selection of racing prints and record shops become stocked with The Dubliners' Greatest Hits.

The hotel business probably benefits above all others as there are never enough beds in the town to satisfy the demand. The big hotels like the Golden Valley and the Queen's are usually booked up a year in advance for most of their rooms and all around the town hotels and bed and breakfast establishments manage to cram just a few more in than they can strictly manage, but nobody complains, certainly not the hotels or the clients who are often happy to get any accommodation for the week. Everyone seems to prosper. The night-clubs put on special events – usually aimed at the male population – and the taxi and bus companies run virtually non-stop.

With the incredible traffic congestion (which is however well managed today by the experienced police force and as good as can be expected), the roads are a nightmare for local people from about midday until the first race and then from the last race for about two hours. Yet even the traffic problems can bring welcome funds for enterprising locals. Some of the pubs with sizeable car parks lay on taxi services to the Racecourse; some, within walking distance of the course, sell car-parking spaces at a daily rate, as do some of the local farmers and landowners. Those unfortunate enough to live in quiet side roads relatively near to the course have to put up with hoards of cars taking up every possible space.

Throughout the week the air is filled with the whirring of helicopters as they come in to land at the course, and at the nearby Gloucestershire Airport (formerly Staverton Airport) extra flights are laid on. As many travel services as possible are provided for the Races, be they buses, coaches, taxis, trains, helicopters or aircraft, and yet there is still always demand for more.

Most locals put up with the traffic problems and invasion of race enthusiasts as par for the course and have learnt to work around them and cope for the few days. Many locals who cannot make a quick profit from the Races still enjoy enormously the great change that comes over the town. There is a definite festival atmosphere in Cheltenham in Races week; the numbers of buskers, the general *joie de vivre* of the Irish and the other racegoers, the amount of outside entertainment so rare at any other time of the year (apart perhaps from the Music and Literature Festivals that are the pride of most Cheltonians) all add up to a great spirit.

Unfortunately and inevitably the downside of this huge party is the crime that follows any crowd, particularly a crowd that swells to the size of that seen at Cheltenham. Pickpockets find easy pickings with people pressed closely together. Shoplifters are as bad but not such a hazard to the general public, and thefts from cars. These all amount to a nightmare world of crime that swarms and festers over the town. Even the hotels and pubs remove many of their usual ornaments and books from shelves that are easily reached and any pictures not screwed to the wall are put away for a few days. Nevertheless the crime element must not be over-emphasized. It is an awful consequence of the Races, but the town benefits so much in so many other ways that it can cope with this negative aspect. The prosperity brought by the Races in so many walks of life, the atmosphere and the occasional famous faces that can be seen amply pay for the traffic problems and the crime, at least for the time being, and so Cheltenham must be very thankful to the Races, for without them it may just have been a one-time Royal Spa without a future in today's world. Instead it is an expanding, modern, internationally famous inland town, known and loved by all race enthusiasts.

At modern Festivals the traffic congestion can be the worst part of the day. Here the former farmland of Prestbury Park Farm is filled to capacity with the cars of race fans. In nearby Bishops Cleeve, Prestbury and Cheltenham all parking spaces and facilities are inevitably taken by racegoers.

Early morning drinkers overflowing from the Crown and Harp on the Cheltenham Road in Bishops Cleeve before making their way to the 1997 Gold Cup meeting. This is a common sight all over the Cheltenham area during Festival week and naturally climaxes on the final day.

On one of her last traditional stops at the Bakery Stores, the Queen Mother is greeted by grocer John Fogarty, with whom she is shaking hands, and Philip Delaney. The tradition of the Queen Mother stopping in Cheltenham began in 1969 when Philip Delaney, who at that time had a grocery business in Leckhampton, suggested to customers that they congregate outside his shop on Gold Cup day at 4.30 p.m. to see the Queen Mother pass by on her way home. Unfortunately the weather was bad and she passed the shop before the expected time. Philip Delaney then wrote to her explaining what had happened and the disappointment of his clients and he was subsequently promised that the royal car would slow down the next year. Not only did the car slow down but it stopped and Philip Delaney was invited to step into the car to meet the Queen Mother. In subsequent years the tradition became established and when the lease on the shop expired in Leckhampton and he moved to the Bakery Stores in Prestbury, owned by John Fogarty, the Queen Mother kindly agreed to make the detour to sustain the wonderful relationship with the town that had been built up.

Off Swindon Lane and less than ½ mile from Prestbury Park is the Wymans Brook estate built in the mid-1960s with many of the roads, closes and drives honouring past equine heroes of Cheltenham – most were winners of either the Gold Cup or the Champion Hurdle. *Arkle* is the most recent winner remembered and *Golden Miller* the oldest.

The Queen's Hotel is still very well patronized by race fans, and is certainly Cheltenham's most famous hotel. It was once the regular venue of the Champion Jockey's dinner, which today is held at the Racecourse itself. First opened in 1838, the hotel is styled on the Temple of Jupiter in Rome.

The Little Owl pub on the Cirencester Road in Charlton Kings, Cheltenham. Originally named after the 1981 Gold Cup winner ridden by Jim Wilson, the trainer now based in Charlton Kings, the pub used to have a sign outside that was a portrait of the horse. Unfortunately the present owners have missed the relevance of the name and the sign has been changed to show a picture of a little owl.

The Dawn Run in Albion Street, Cheltenham, named after that wonderful mare which won both the Gold Cup and the Champion Hurdle before her tragic death in France.

The sign for the modernized Garrison Savannah Suite at the King's Head in Bishops Cleeve. Having local owners, *Garrison Savannah* was really taken to heart by the people of Cheltenham and there were great celebrations when he won the Gold Cup in 1991.

The National Hunt public house on the corner of Benhall Avenue and Whittington Road in Cheltenham, named quite obviously after the Festival that has made Cheltenham internationally famous.

In Devon Avenue is the Golden Miller pub, honouring the Dorothy Paget-owned horse that monopolized the Gold Cup in the mid-1930s.

THE LOCAL CONNNECTION

Almost from their inception in the early nineteenth century Cheltenham Races have had very strong local links. The Holman and Nicholson heritage has already been documented and gives a clear indication of how important a local nucleus of talent was to the success of the Races and of National Hunt in the town. That incredible base is best seen in the Grand National results. If we assume that the first Grand National was in 1839 (thus discounting the 'Maghull Grand Nationals'), then in the first thirty-six years exactly one third of the winning jockeys in the race came from or had origins in Cheltenham. 'Black' Tom Oliver won three: on *Gay Lad* in 1842, *Vanguard* in 1843 and *Peter Simple* in 1853 (he also won one of the two Maghull races, on *Sir Henry* in 1838). George Stevens won a record five, as has already been outlined earlier in the book, and William Archer won in 1858 on the William Holman-trained *Little Charlie*. Thomas Pickernell, the contemporary of Adam Lindsay Gordon at Cheltenham College, under the assumed name of Mr Thomas, won three (of the incredible seventeen in which he rode) – 1860 on *Anatis*, 1871 with *The Lamb* and 1875 on *The Pathfinder*.

The influence of these men did not end there. Thomas Pickernell went on to become the first National Hunt Inspector of Courses. The contribution made by George Stevens, William Archer and William Holman in raising interest in horse racing in Cheltenham was considerable, and Tom Oliver had a most profound effect.

Oliver's nickname, 'Black' Tom Oliver, possibly refers to his swarthy skin, his frequenting of debtors' prison or his reputed dubious tactics in winning a steeplechase at Warwick (the race was run during a snowstorm and he allegedly used the poor visibility to hide behind a haystack on the first circuit, rejoining the race on the second to romp home). A contemporary of William Holman, he was clearly a talented jockey and afterwards a trainer, not just of horses but also of men. He taught George Stevens much of what he knew and also took Adam Lindsay Gordon and Thomas Pickernell under his wing. When he died on 8 January 1874 he had already outlived two of his most famous pupils, Stevens and Gordon.

As the popularity of racing waned towards the end of the nineteenth century so did the number of racing folk in the town, but in the 1920s, when the National Hunt Festival was coming into its own, the town veritably exploded with equestrian interest, and for a period of perhaps thirty to forty years Bishops Cleeve, Cleeve Hill, Woodmancote and in particular Prestbury were home to some of the biggest names in racing. At one time in the 1920s the great jockeys Tim Hamey, Billy Stott and Billy Speck were neighbours in Bishops Cleeve. A contemporary of theirs, Gerry Wilson, also lived in Cheltenham and like Hamey went on to train with considerable success. This was also the time of Frenchie Nicholson, Davy Jones (apprenticing in Prestbury at Morningside Stables in Mill Street with Ben Roberts) and Charlie Piggott (training in the old Holman stables, Cleeve Lodge), who turned out *African Sister* to win the 1939 Champion Hurdle.

When Frenchie Nicholson was training in Prestbury in the 1950s and '60s he was contemporary with Tim Hamey, training in Park Lane, Prestbury, Phil Doherty, and John Roberts (the son of Ben Roberts), who worked from the Prestbury Court Stables – John Roberts trained the only locally trained winner of the Gold Cup, *Four Ten* in 1954.

Prestbury was at this time the equivalent of what Lambourn is today, a racing village with apprentice jockeys in lodgings and the clatter of hooves ringing on the village roads in the early morning as the horses were led up on to Cleeve Hill for their exercise. In those heady days many great names of riding were serving their apprenticeships with one or other of the trainers and it was these young lads who would often be seen taking the horses out and bringing them back in. Rex Hamey, Paul Cook, Pat Eddery, David Nicholson and Walter Swinburn were some of those young lads, some following in their father's footsteps, some coming all the way from Ireland to apprentice specifically in Prestbury. Some would be flat race legends; some would reap their rewards in National Hunt.

Unfortunately as these trainers retired from racing the new generation of trainers did not want to fill their shoes, choosing instead to have stables with more open space around them. When Frenchie Nicholson retired in 1979 Prestbury was no longer the haven for racing folk it had once been.

Jim Wilson kept up some tradition of local success which culminated in 1981 with his winning ride on *Little Owl* in the Gold Cup, and he now trains in Charlton Kings where he has fifteen horses in his stable. He is conveniently close to the West Down of Cleeve Hill and uses the gallops on the original racecourse for his horses' exercise.

Cleeve Lodge is kept alive by Owen O'Neill who, after working for Bill Marshall when he trained there, later bought the house and stables for himself. He has trained there ever since with some success. Norman Babbage, one of the new names in racehorse training, also currently trains on the hill, with his base at Cleeve Cloud, Nutterswood, but he is expecting to move to new facilities at Brockhampton, still only a stone's throw from the Racecourse, where there will be stabling for up to thirty horses and where he will have his own gallops as well as being close enough to Cleeve Hill to use that if necessary. Postlip Racing, nestling at the base of Cleeve Hill on the Winchcombe side, is a new establishment aiming to keep the great Cheltenham tradition alive.

Although the number of trainers, jockeys and owners in Cheltenham and its environs today is nowhere near as great as it once was, it is because Cheltenham had, at crucial times in its history, a good racing base that the success and survival of the Races were assured. Now that the Races are very firmly established they can afford to have less of a local base, but for tradition's sake it is hoped that some sort of local representation of National Hunt training remains here forever.

The Cheltenham Grand Annual Steeplechase of 1926 with Bishops Cleeve jockey, Tim Hamey, leading on *Black Miner*. Trained by J. Dodd and owned by H.S. Kenyon, *Black Miner* went on to win the race.

Tim Hamey well out in front on *Black Miner*, 1926. *Jargoon* with F. Rees finished second in the steeplechase and *Clashing Arms*, ridden by Jack Anthony, was third.

Tim Hamey, on the right, talking to S.T. Freeman, the owner of *Free Choice*, the horse that Tim had just trained to win the Winchcombe Selling Handicap Steeplechase, 28 December 1938. After a very successful riding career Tim turned to training in 1938, basing his operation first in Bishops Cleeve, then, after a spell in the army, in Prestbury at Moat Farm, Park Lane. The jockey of *Free Choice* on this occasion was Frenchie Nicholson who later followed Tim Hamey's lead to train from Prestbury. *Montclair*, ridden by W. Parvin, finished second in the race and *Tit for Tat* with Lord Roderic Pratt took third.

Two great names in National Hunt history, Davy Jones on the left and Tim Hamey in the middle, both former winning Gold Cup jockeys. Tim Hamey won on *Koko* in 1926 and Davy Jones at the age of thirty-seven on the Lord Stalbridge-owned and trained *Red Rower* in 1945 (to date this is the only winner of the Gold Cup trained by its owner). Born in Wales, Davy Jones was apprenticed by Ben Roberts in Prestbury and after a very successful career riding over jumps he turned to flat racing at the age of forty, continuing to race for the next twenty-five years.

The Gentleman of Cheltenham. Tim Hamey in his retirement kneels on the right at the George Stevens memorial in Southam with other notable names of racing. Tim's son, Rex, followed in his father's footsteps both as a jockey and as a trainer. Tim Hamey passed away on Easter Sunday, 15 April 1990 and is buried in Bishops Cleeve churchyard.

Peter Doherty up on a horse trained by Phil Doherty from his stables in Prestbury, being led by Richard Pitman at Worcester.

Peter Dever on *Rig Steel*, trailing Grand National winner, *West Tip*, over one of Cheltenham's jumps. The horse later threw Peter at Newbury, resulting in his breaking an arm and an ankle. Based at Badsey near Evesham during his riding career, Peter Dever now owns Peaks and Troughs in Andover Road, Cheltenham, a shop catering for all the needs of horse owners. As a jockey he won the 1984 Postlip Chase at Cheltenham on *Arctic Beau*.

Jim Wilson on *Willie Wumpkins* during one of his trio of Coral Golden Hurdle Finals between 1979 and 1981. *Willie Wumpkins* was owned by Jane Pilkington, the wife of T.D. 'Boy' Pilkington, and they subsequently became the in-laws of Jim Wilson. As an amateur jockey Jim Wilson rode 205 winners and in 1985 turned to training from his stables at the base of Ham Hill in Charlton Kings. His first Cheltenham winner was, quite appropriately, in the 1987 Coral Golden Hurdle Final with *Taberna Lord*.

There is horse racing throughout his family. His great-aunt was Mrs D. Beddington who owned the 1965 Champion Hurdle winner, *Kirriemuir*, ridden by G.W. Robinson and trained by Fulke Walwyn, and his aunt on his mother's side married the great jockey and trainer, Fred Winter. Even his mother was a winning owner at Cheltenham with *Herring Gull*.

Right Wing at Worcester Racecourse, the first winner for Cleeve Hill-based trainer, Owen O'Neill. O'Neill turned to training after a successful riding career during which he was twice Irish Apprentice Champion Jockey (with more than 300 wins in his first three years). As a professional jockey from 1955 to 1965 he rode seventy-five winners on the flat and twenty winners over hurdles.

King of the Winds, the winner of the Wills Castella Hurdle Race for Owen O'Neill at Cheltenham. O'Neill obtained his trainer's licence in April 1966. He worked for a while under Bill Marshall at Cleeve Lodge, moved to Cirencester to work with Hugh Ellis, and came back to Cleeve Lodge in 1969 as owner. He also trained *Moleboard* who won the Woodmancote Novices' Hurdle on 1 January 1988. He was very fancied for the Sun Alliance Hurdle of 1988 but got kicked in the stomach by *Another Schedule* and broke a rib. Owen O'Neill has also had success with *Celtic Bob* and *Stormy Prospect* and on 10 August 1993 at Bath he secured an incredible 3,416–1 double on the flat. He has currently got twenty horses in his stable and continues the great racing tradition at Cleeve Lodge on Cleeve Hill.

The last great Cheltenham winning horse to have Cheltenham connections, *Garrison Savannah* (centre), ridden by Mark Pitman on his way to winning the 1988–89 Coral Golden Hurdle qualifier. Second was *Inde Pulse* and third was *Sooner Still*.

Mark Pitman and *Garrison Savannah* winning the Coral Golden Hurdle. Ridden by Ben de Haan, *Garrison Savannah* went on to win the 1990 Sun Alliance Chase and then, with Mark Pitman in the saddle again, the 1991 Gold Cup.

Garrison Savannah being led by his owners after winning the 1988 Coral Golden Hurdle qualifier at Cheltenham with Mark Pitman in the saddle. The horse is particularly important to Cheltenham as it is owned by Autofour Engineering of Alstone Lane. The partners in the company, Roger Voysey, Malcolm Burdock and John Davies (former Cheltenham Town footballer), bought the horse in 1986 for £7,500. When he was retired in November 1996 he had won nine of his fifty races and £229,223 in prize money. He was named after a racetrack in Barbados and was trained throughout his career by Jenny Pitman with whom he still works, acting as a hack for her stables at Lambourn.

CHELTENHAM RACECOURSE
TODAY

T he success of racing in Cheltenham is due in no small part to the wonderful condition in which the course is maintained and to the diligent work of the fence and hurdle makers who construct and maintain the very best obstacles for the horses to jump. On the two main courses at Cheltenham – the old and new courses, both of which are still used – there are twenty-nine fences, some with ditches, some water jumps and some just fences. They are made of natural materials, timber, birch and gorse. Timber rots in the ground, birch becomes brittle and shrinks over time and the fences experience some considerable wear during races. Therefore, they have to be rebuilt every two to three years. The timber acts as the frame for the fences with the birch being the main body and the gorse packed tightly over the birch in the front. The minimum height of the fences is 4½ ft so new fences are constructed a little higher at about 4 ft 7½ in to 4 ft 8 in to allow for the loss of about an inch during the season.

Today there are sixteen days of racing at Cheltenham each season. There is now a Sunday race meet in November and the last race meeting of the season is usually an evening meeting in April. These meetings attract an annual crowd of over 250,000, the vast majority of whom come for the Festival – 59,488 came through the gates on the 1997 Gold Cup day alone. The Murphy's meeting is the next best patronized, followed by the New Year's Day meet and then the evening meeting at the end of the season.

This leaves a large proportion of the year when the Racecourse is not utilized for racing, but under the command of Cheltenham's Managing Director, Edward Gillespie, the Racecourse remains a focal point throughout the year. This massive resource of land and buildings is so well managed that it is rarely out of use. On Sundays there is an outside market and car boot sale. The hard standing just off New Barn Lane is used for out of town parking each Saturday with a bus ferrying shoppers into Cheltenham. The buildings are hired out for book and antique fairs. Wedding receptions, dinner-dances and corporate functions are all catered for in the Prestbury Suite. The Caravan Club has a site on the course. Add these uses to all the other occasional attractions, such as circuses, that utilize the space, and the whole of Prestbury Park has been transformed into a profitable commodity. This optimum utilization of resources must be heralded as one of the most important features of the modern Racecourse and a great achievement by Edward Gillespie. The Racecourse is a business and needs to be run as one. Yet, by encouraging people to visit the Racecourse for attractions so totally unrelated to racing, such events also make the Racecourse more accessible which naturally encourages local people to go to the Races.

The modernization of the Racecourse stands began shortly before the arrival of Edward Gillespie in 1979. Almost twenty years later that modernization programme has just about been completed, with the latest phase, the construction of the new Tattersall's Grandstand at a cost of approximately £10 million, being finished in time for the 1997 Festival. Since 1979 the Racecourse has spent almost £30 million on redevelopment, including the redevelopment of the Club Stand, the Winners' Enclosure, the Parade Ring and the construction of a new stableyard as well as the Tattersall's Grandstand.

This development has been necessary not just because the old facilities were deteriorating, but also because of the increased popularity of Cheltenham. Today, during the Festival Week, about 150,000 people can be expected through the gates (from 1998 the numbers attending the Festival will be strictly limited to 50,000 per day). Catered for by the racecourse caterer, Letheby & Christopher, with their 3,000 waiters, bar staff and cooks, they will consume approximately 14,000 gallons of Guinness, 2,700 gallons of champagne, 40,000 hamburgers and hot dogs and one ton of salmon. Approximately 5,000 Irish racegoers travel over to Cheltenham which brings business not only to Cheltenham but also to airports and ferry companies – all of which put on extra services each year for the Irish invasion. The number of horses racing at the Festival has increased in recent years; today around 400 horses will take part in the 20 races. These horses attracted over £25 million in bets on the course in 1997 and the total prize money was over £1 million.

Inevitably, with more people being attracted to the course, there is need for greater security and more restrictions have to be made on the public's freedom. Today people are not allowed to walk the course before Festival races and, following the *Imperial Call* Gold Cup win of 1996 when overzealous fans pushed their way into the winners' enclosure, completely swamping the horse, jockey and connections, there are now more security men (twenty in 1997 as opposed to twelve in 1996) around the parade ring and tighter controls ensuring that the occasion is not spoilt for all the spectators – now if anyone trespasses into the winners' enclosure he or she can expect to be ejected from the whole course.

With the Festival televised not just by Britain's Channel Four but by television crews from all over the world it is important that the sporting arena gives the impression of professionalism and good management, as well as projecting the atmosphere of a great sporting occasion. This is what it does and as long as it is blessed with the great management it has experienced under the ownership of the Racecourse Holdings Trust then there is no reason to suspect that it will ever change.

As the millennium approaches, restoration work by the Gloucestershire Warwickshire Railway on the Racecourse station and its line is at such a point that, providing the volunteer labour, financial backing and assistance, like that already provided by Westbury Homes and Anglia Water, continue, the station should be open for use by Gold Cup Day in the year 2000. This would surely be a classic mix of past and present: a great modern sporting arena graced by that romantic spectacle of a steam railway – a fabulous way to travel to the races.

Cheltenham Racecourse as seen from the stands. In the immediate foreground is the Members' Lawn and the last fences are just beyond it.

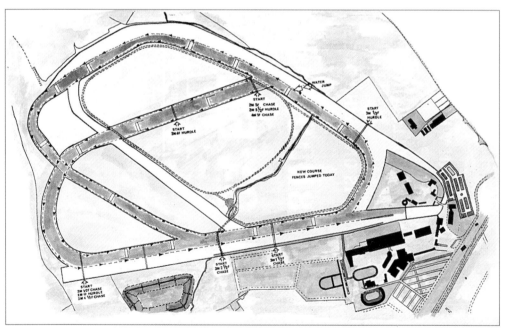

The New Course, which was first set out and used for the 1965 Gold Cup. There have been many alterations to the course over the last forty years. In 1958 the old National Hunt Course which ran behind the stands, adjacent to the railway line, was closed and a new shute was added. In 1976 a section which had included the start of the Gold Cup race was closed and 1980 saw a section around the course enclosure closed. The Park Course was opened in 1991.

One of Cheltenham's water jumps.

The ditch at fence twelve.

Fence twelve. Its ditch with the jump board is clearly visible to jockeys and horses as they approach.

The last fence at Cheltenham.

George Excell, the former head fence builder at Cheltenham, at the last fence. He still plays a very active part in the fence building and maintenance operation at Cheltenham.

Keith Jones, the present head fence builder, after a particularly cold night during the Cheltenham Festival, trying to clear one of the water jumps of the ice that has formed.

The racecourse stables were built in 1993. There are 202 stables in the yard which also has a veterinary examination room and equine store. Many of the stable doors bear the name of the Gold Cup or Champion Hurdle winner stabled there before victory. During the Festival it is common for about 60 Irish horses to be stabled here for the duration of the meeting, and in total approximately 400 horses use the stables over the three days. Security is very tight with plenty of close circuit cameras in action twenty-four hours per day when the stables are in use and a guard to keep a watchful eye on the monitors. During the Festival there are five Jockey Club security people in the stableyard walking around and keeping a general watch over everything. These modern stables are built on the same site as the original wooden stables.

On the left is Lord Vestey, the present chairman of Cheltenham Racecourse, and standing on the right is Maj. Phillip Arkwright, the clerk of the course. (*photograph reproduced by kind permission of Bernard Parkin*)

The staff of Cheltenham Racecourse with the flag presented to them on 7 October 1994 when Cheltenham won the Racecourse of the Year Award. On the far right stands Edward Gillespie, the managing director of Cheltenham, who was in charge of his first Cheltenham Festival in 1980.

Peter McNeile, the commercial manager at Cheltenham Racecourse.

The statue of *Dawn Run* and Jonjo O'Neill looking over the parade ring and winners' enclosure at Cheltenham with the grandstand on the left. The Royal Box is situated on the end of the grandstand nearest to the camera and is regularly home to members of the Royal Family as they come and enjoy the racing. The top two levels of this part of the grandstand are just for private viewing and corporate rooms.

The parade ring and winners' enclosure with the weighing room just visible on the left. The new parade ring was opened in 1982; the terracing has a capacity for approximately 4,000.

Taking down the temporary stands that were part of the Guinness Village, erected to cope with the extra requirements of the 1997 Festival. The tented village adds an extra 10,000 per day to the capacity of the Racecourse.

Construction of the new Tattersall's Grandstand underway. The constructors, John Mowlem & Co. plc, have a long and impressive history dating back almost 200 years to 1808 when a stonemason from Swanage named John Mowlem moved to London to find work. In 1822 he had his own business as a mason and by 1830 he and his business partners were contracted to repave the streets of London. Today the company is one of the largest and most successful construction companies in the United Kingdom, having worked on such impressive projects as the stadia for Tottenham Hotspur FC, Aston Villa FC and Twickenham.

Work on the new grandstand well underway. In July 1995 John Mowlem & Co. plc were appointed as contractor designate for the £10 million project of demolishing the existing Tattersall's Grandstand and replacing it with a modern grandstand that would incorporate a panoramic restaurant, bars and hospitality boxes. Construction was not due to commence for another nine months but the Racecourse wanted Mowlem to become an integral part of the whole project, taking part in the decision-making process and advising on design, materials and construction techniques.

The first panel of glass is in place for the panoramic restaurant in the top left-hand corner of the building. A special 'Planar' frameless glazing system was utilized which allows a totally unimpeded view of the Racecourse. The general structure of the grandstand is made of structural steel and precast concrete. (*photograph reproduced by kind permission of Mr P. Jackson*)

The finished grandstand from the side. Construction was carried out between the 1996 and 1997 Cheltenham Festivals over a period of about forty-seven weeks. The bottom three tiers of the grandstand were open for the January 1997 race meeting and the top two tiers were opened in time for the Festival, fully and lavishly furnished. The stand was designed by the Lobb Partnership, the architects for Cheltenham's previous development projects.

The new entrance to the Racecourse's Hall of Fame and to the new Tattersall's Grandstand.

Cheltenham Racecourse's Hall of Fame was originally opened in 1993, but with the construction of the new stand it was doubled in size for the 1997 Festival. This is a permanent exhibition, open to the public, that charts the history of steeplechasing and of Cheltenham Racecourse. Suspended from the ceiling are the names of all the Gold Cup winners along with the colours of the jockeys who rode them. Most aspects of modern and past racing life are illustrated by way of exhibits, videos and pictorial displays. Homage is paid to the many heroes and heroines who have made racing and, in particular, Cheltenham what it is. There is even a mechanical horse that simulates a steeplechase ride. Currently the Hall of Fame is the only exhibition in Great Britain dedicated to National Hunt racing.

The Tattersall's Betting Hall on the first level of the New Tattersall's Grandstand. The hall includes a tote, an on-course betting shop and easy accessibility to the bookmakers in front of the stands on racedays.

The Winged Ox Bar on level two of the new stand is designed with a Celtic theme. As with all of the lower three floors, this bar was first opened in time for the January 1997 meeting.

Level four of the new Racecourse building. On the right are the two glass lift doors which operate to all five levels; on the left are directions to the hospitality boxes. On the back wall is a version of the painting of the 1826 Cleeve Hill Races (see page 12).

The spectacular panoramic restaurant on level five of the new grandstand. The restaurant seats up to 300 people and is situated directly opposite the winning post of the course, giving an unassailable viewpoint for racegoers. Tables also have their own televisions so that diners can keep fully in touch with all that is going on beneath them on the course. During Festival Week the restaurant charges £345 per head and for its inaugural Festival it was sold out many weeks in advance.

Fully completed by early February, in time for the 1997 Festival, the New Tattersall's Grandstand increased the floor space at the Racecourse by half as much again. The all-seater upper level (beneath the windowed panoramic restaurant) accommodates 700 and beneath it are standing tiers for spectators.

Gold Cup Day, Thursday 13 March 1997. The new grandstand is in full use, brimming to capacity for a record-breaking festival. Over 150,000 came through the turnstiles during the three days and on Gold Cup Day a record 59,488 crowded in. Martin Pipe was the most successful trainer with four wins over the three days, and the London Clubs Trophy for the jockey with the most wins went to Tony McCoy who rode three winners, including the Gold Cup–Champion Hurdle double on *Mr Mulligan* and *Make a Stand* respectively.

APPENDICES

Graham Isom's painting of the 1993 Gold Cup race with Jodami *on the left and* Rushing Wild *on the right.*

THE SMURFIT
CHAMPION HURDLE

CHELTENHAM

16TH MARCH, 1993

CHAMPION HURDLE WINNERS

Year	Winner	Jockey	Trainer
1927	*Blaris*	G. Duller	W. Payne
1928	*Brown Jack*	L.B. Rees	A. Hastings
1929	*Royal Falcon*	F.B. Rees	R. Gore
1930	*Brown Tony*	T. Cullinan	J. Anthony
1931	No race because of frost		
1932	*Insurance*	T. Leader	B. Briscoe
1933	*Insurance*	W. Stott	B. Briscoe
1934	*Chenango*	D. Morgan	I. Anthony
1935	*Lion Courage*	G. Wilson	F.A. Brown
1936	*Victor Norman*	H. Nicholson	M. Blair
1937	*Free Fare*	G. Pellerin	E. Gwilt
1938	*Our Hope*	Capt. P. Harding	R. Gubbins
1939	*African Sister*	K. Piggott	C. Piggott
1940	*Solford*	S. Magee	O. Anthony
1941	*Seneca*	R. Smyth	V. Smyth
1942	*Forestation*	R. Smyth	V. Smyth
1943	No race because of war		
1944	No race because of war		
1945	*Brains Trust*	T.F. Rimell	G. Wilson
1946	*Distel*	R. O'Ryan	M. Arnott
1947	*National Spirit*	D. Morgan	V. Smyth
1948	*National Spirit*	R. Smyth	V. Smyth
1949	*Hatton's Grace*	A. Brabazon	M.V. O'Brien
1950	*Hatton's Grace*	A. Brabazon	M.V. O'Brien
1951	*Hatton's Grace*	T. Molony	M.V. O'Brien
1952	*Sir Ken*	T. Molony	W. Stephenson
1953	*Sir Ken*	T. Molony	W. Stephenson

1954	*Sir Ken*	T. Molony	W. Stephenson
1955	*Clair Soleil*	F.T. Winter	H.R. Price
1956	*Doorknocker*	H. Sprague	W. Hall
1957	*Merry Deal*	G. Underwood	A. Jones
1958	*Bandalore*	G. Slack	S. Wright
1959	*Fare Time*	F.T. Winter	H.R. Price
1960	*Another Flash*	H. Beasley	P. Sleator
1961	*Eborneezer*	F.T. Winter	H.R. Price
1962	*Anzio*	G. Robinson	F.T. Walwyn
1963	*Winning Fair*	A. Lillingston	G. Spencer
1964	*Magic Court*	P. McCarron	T. Robson
1965	*Kirriemuir*	G. Robinson	F.T. Walwyn
1966	*Salmon Spray*	J. Haine	R. Turnell
1967	*Saucy Kit*	R. Edwards	M.H. Easterby
1968	*Persian War*	J. Uttley	C. Davies
1969	*Persian War*	J. Uttley	C. Davies
1970	*Persian War*	J. Uttley	C. Davies
1971	*Bula*	P. Kelleway	F.T. Winter
1972	*Bula*	P. Kelleway	F.T. Winter
1973	*Comedy of Errors*	W. Smith	T.F. Rimell
1974	*Lanzarote*	R. Pitman	F.T. Winter
1975	*Comedy of Errors*	K. White	T.F. Rimell
1976	*Night Nurse*	P. Broderick	M.H. Easterby
1977	*Night Nurse*	P. Broderick	M.H. Easterby
1978	*Monksfield*	T. Kinane	D. McDonough
1979	*Monksfield*	D.T. Hughes	D. McDonough
1980	*Sea Pigeon*	J.J. O'Neill	M.H. Easterby
1981	*Sea Pigeon*	J. Francome	M.H. Easterby
1982	*For Auction*	M.C. Magnier	M. Cunnigham
1983	*Gaye Brief*	R. Linley	Mrs M. Rimell
1984	*Dawn Run*	J.J. O'Neill	P. Mullins
1985	*See You Then*	S. Smith-Eccles	N. Henderson
1986	*See You Then*	S. Smith-Eccles	N. Henderson
1987	*See You Then*	S. Smith-Eccles	N. Henderson
1988	*Celtic Shot*	P. Scudamore	F.T. Winter
1989	*Beech Road*	R. Guest	G.B. Balding
1990	*Kribensis*	R. Dunwoody	M. Stoute
1991	*Morley Street*	J. Frost	G.B. Balding
1992	*Royal Gait*	G. McCourt	J. Fanshawe
1993	*Granville Again*	P. Scudamore	M.C.Pipe
1994	*Flakey Dove*	M. Dwyer	R. Price
1995	*Alderbrook*	N. Williamson	K. Bailey
1996	*Collier Bay*	G. Bradley	J. Old
1997	*Make a Stand*	A. McCoy	M.C. Pipe

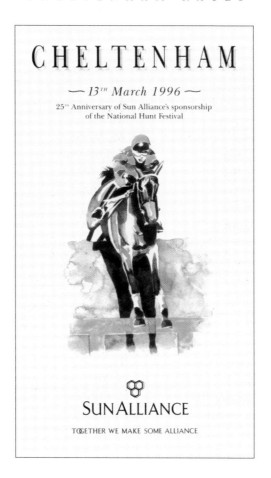

THE QUEEN MOTHER CHAMPION CHASE WINNERS

The 2-mile Champion Chase was first run in the 1959 March Festival. In 1980 the Queen Mother graciously permitted the race to be renamed in her honour.

Year	Winner	Jockey	Trainer
1959	*Quita Que*	J. Cox	D. Moore
1960	*Fortria*	P. Taaffe	T.W. Dreaper
1961	*Fortria*	P. Taaffe	T.W. Dreaper
1962	*Piperton*	D.V. Dick	A.H. Tomlinson
1963	*Sandy Abbot*	S. Mellor	G.R. Owen
1964	*Ben Stack*	P. Taaffe	T.W. Dreaper
1965	*Dunkirk*	D.V. Dick	P. Cazalet
1966	*Flyingbolt*	P. Taaffe	T.W. Dreaper
1967	*Drinny's Double*	F. Nash	R. Turnbull
1968	*Drinny's Double*	F. Nash	R. Turnbull
1969	*Muir*	B. Hannon	T.W. Dreaper
1970	*Straight Fort*	P. Taaffe	T.W. Dreaper

1971	*Crisp*	P. Kelleway	F.T. Winter
1972	*Royal Relief*	W. Smith	E. Courage
1973	*Inkslinger*	T. Carberry	D. Moore
1974	*Royal Relief*	W. Smith	E. Courage
1975	*Lough Inagh*	S. Barker	J. Dreaper
1976	*Skymas*	M. Morris	J. Lusk
1977	*Skymas*	M. Morris	J. Lusk
1978	*Hilly Way*	T. Carmody	P. McCreery
1979	*Hilly Way*	T.M. Walsh	P. McCreery
1980	*Chinrullah**	D. Hughes	M. O'Toole
1981	*Drumgora*	F. Berry	A. Moore
1982	*Rathgorman*	K. Whyte	M. Dickinson
1983	*Badsworth Boy*	R. Earnshaw	M. Dickinson
1984	*Badsworth Boy*	R. Earnshaw	M. Dickinson
1985	*Badsworth Boy*	R. Earnshaw	Mrs M. Dickinson
1986	*Buck House*	T. Carmody	M. Morris (Ire)
1987	*Pearlyman*	P. Scudamore	J. Edwards
1988	*Pearlyman*	T. Morgan	J. Edwards
1989	*Barnbrook Again*	S. Sherwood	D. Elsworth
1990	*Barnbrook Again*	H. Davies	D. Elsworth
1991	*Katabatic*	S. McNeill	A. Turnell
1992	*Remittance Man*	J. Osborne	N. Henderson
1993	*Deep Sensation*	D. Murphy	J. Gifford
1994	*Viking Flagship*	A. Maguire	D. Nicholson
1995	*Viking Flagship*	C. Swan	D. Nicholson
1996	*Klairon Davis*	F. Woods	A.L.T. Moore
1997	*Martha's Son*	R. Farrant	T. Forster

*Subsequently disqualified on technical grounds.
Another Dolly was then installed as winner.

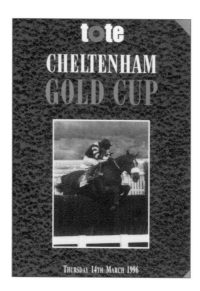

CHELTENHAM GOLD CUP WINNERS

Year	Winner	Jockey	Trainer
1924	*Red Splash*	F. Rees	F.E. Worthington
1925	*Ballinode*	E. Leader	F. Morgan
1926	*Koko*	J. Hamey	A. Bickley
1927	*Thrown In*	Hon. H. Grosvenor	O. Anthony
1928	*Patron Saint*	F. Rees	H. Harrison
1929	*Easter Hero*	F. Rees	J. Anthony
1930	*Easter Hero*	T. Cullinan	J. Anthony
1931	No race because of frost		
1932	*Golden Miller*	T. Leader	B. Briscoe
1933	*Golden Miller*	W. Stott	B. Briscoe
1934	*Golden Miller*	G. Wilson	B. Briscoe
1935	*Golden Miller*	G. Wilson	B. Briscoe
1936	*Golden Miller*	E. Williams	O. Anthony
1937	Race abandoned because of snow		
1938	*Morse Code*	D. Morgan	I. Anthony
1939	*Brendan's Cottage*	G. Owen	G. Beeby
1940	*Roman Hackle*	E. Williams	O. Anthony
1941	*Poet Prince*	R. Burford	I. Anthony
1942	*Medoc II*	H. Nicholson	R. Hobbs
1943	No race because of war		
1944	No race because of war		
1945	*Red Rower*	D.L. Jones	Lord Stalbridge
1946	*Prince Regent*	T. Hyde	T.W. Dreaper
1947	*Fortina*	R. Black	H. Christie
1948	*Cottage Rake*	A. Brabazon	M.V. O'Brien
1949	*Cottage Rake*	A. Brabazon	M.V. O'Brien
1950	*Cottage Rake*	A. Brabazon	M.V. O'Brien
1951	*Silver Fame*	M. Malony	G. Beeby

1952	*Mont Tremblant*	D.V. Dick	F. Walwyn
1953	*Knock Hard*	T. Malony	M.V. O'Brien
1954	*Four Ten*	T. Cusack	J. Roberts
1955	*Gay Donald*	A. Grantham	J. Ford
1956	*Limber Hill*	J. Power	W. Dutton
1957	*Linwell*	M. Scudamore	C. Mallon
1958	*Kerstin*	S. Hayhurst	Maj. C. Bewicke
1959	*Roddy Owen*	H. Beasley	D.J. Morgan
1960	*Pas Seul*	W. Rees	R. Turnell
1961	*Saffron Tartan*	F.T. Winter	D. Butchers
1962	*Mandarin*	F.T. Winter	F. Walwyn
1963	*Mill House*	G.W. Robinson	F. Walwyn
1964	*Arkle*	P. Taaffe	T.W. Dreaper
1965	*Arkle*	P. Taaffe	T.W. Dreaper
1966	*Arkle*	P. Taaffe	T.W. Dreaper
1967	*Woodland Venture*	T.W. Biddlecombe	T.F. Rimell
1968	*Fort Leney*	P. Taaffe	T.W. Dreaper
1969	*What a Myth*	P. Kelleway	Ryan Price
1970	*L'Escargot*	T. Carberry	D.L. Moore
1971	*L'Escargot*	T. Carberry	D.L. Moore
1972	*Glencaraig Lady*	F. Berry	F. Flood
1973	*The Dikler*	R. Barry	F. Walwyn
1974	*Captain Christy*	H. Beasley	P. Taaffe
1975	*Ten Up*	T. Carberry	J. Dreaper
1976	*Royal Frolic*	J. Burke	T.F. Rimell
1977	*Davy Lad*	D.T. Hughes	M. O'Toole
1978	*Midnight Court*	J. Francome	F.T. Winter
1979	*Alverton*	J.J. O'Neill	M.H. Easterby
1980	*Tied Cottage**	T. Carberry	D. Moore
1981	*Little Owl*	A.J. Wilson	M.H. Easterby
1982	*Silver Buck*	R. Earnshaw	M. Dickinson
1983	*Bregawn*	G. Bradley	M. Dickinson
1984	*Burrough Hill Lad*	P. Tuck	Mrs J. Pitman
1985	*Forgive 'n' Forget*	M. Dwyer	J. Fitzgerald
1986	*Dawn Run*	J.J. O'Neill	P. Mullins
1987	*The Thinker*	R. Lamb	W.A. Stephenson
1988	*Charter Party*	R. Dunwoody	D. Nicholson
1989	*Desert Orchid*	S. Sherwood	D. Elsworth
1990	*Norton's Coin*	G. McCourt	S.G. Griffiths
1991	*Garrison Savannah*	M. Pitman	Mrs J. Pitman
1992	*Cool Ground*	A. Maguire	T. Balding
1993	*Jodami*	M. Dwyer	P. Beaumont
1994	*The Fellow*	A. Kondrat	F. Doumen
1995	*Master Oats*	N. Williamson	K.C. Bailey
1996	*Imperial Call*	C. O'Dwyer	F. Sutherland
1997	*Mr Mulligan*	A.P. McCoy	N.T. Chance

*Subsequently disqualified for failing a dope test. *Master Smudge* was then installed as the winner.

THE 'NOVEMBER' GOLD CUP HANDICAP CHASE

Year	Winner	Jockey	Trainer

HENNESSEY GOLD CUP

Year	Winner	Jockey	Trainer
1957	*Mandarin*	P. Madden	F. Walwyn
1958	*Taxidermist*	J. Lawrence	F. Walwyn
1959	*Kerstin*	S. Hayhurst	Maj. C. Bewicke

MACKESON GOLD CUP

Year	Winner	Jockey	Trainer
1960	*Fortria*	P. Taaffe	T.W. Dreaper
1961	*Scottish Memories*	C. Finnegan	A. Thomas
1962	*Fortria*	P. Taaffe	T.W. Dreaper
1963	*Richard of Bordeaux*	H. Beasley	F. Walwyn
1964	*Super Flash*	S. Mellor	F. Cundell
1965	*Dunkirk*	W. Rees	P. Cazalet
1966	*Pawnbroker*	P. Broderick	W. Stephenson
1967	*Charlie Worcester*	J. Gifford	H.R. Price
1968	*Jupiter Boy*	E. Harty	T.F. Rimell
1969	*Gay Trip*	T.W. Biddlecombe	T.F. Rimell
1970	*Chatham*	K.B. White	T.F. Rimell
1971	*Gay Trip*	T.W. Biddlecombe	T.F. Rimell
1972	*Red Candle*	J. Fox	Lt. Col. G.R.A Vallance
1973	*Skymas*	T.S. Murphy	J.B. Lusk
1974	*Bruslee*	A. Turnell	M.J. Scudamore
1975	*Clear Cut*	D. Greaves	M. Camacho
1976	*Cancello*	D. Atkins	Capt. N.F. Crump
1977	*Bachelor's Hall*	M. O'Halloran	P.D. Cundell
1978	*Bawnogues*	C. Smith	M. Tate
1979	*Man Alive*	R. Barry	G.W. Richards
1980	*Bright Highway*	G. Newman	M.J.P. O'Brien
1981	*Henry Kissinger*	P. Barton	D.R. Gandolfo
1982	*Fifty Dollars More*	R. Linley	F.T. Winter
1983	*Pounentes*	N. Doughty	W.W. McGhie
1984	*Half Free*	R. Linley	F.T. Winter
1985	*Half Free*	R. Linley	F.T. Winter
1986	*Very Promising*	R. Dunwoody	D. Nicholson
1987	*Beau Ranger*	M. Perrett	M.C. Pipe
1988	*Pegwell Bay*	P. Scudamore	T.A. Foster
1989	*Joint Sovereignty*	G. McCourt	P.J. Hobbs
1990	*Multum in Parvo*	N. Williamson	J.A.C. Edwards
1991	*Another Coral*	R. Dunwoody	D. Nicholson
1992	*Tipping Tim*	C. Llewellyn	N.A. Twiston-Davies
1993	*Bradbury Star*	D. Murphy	J. Gifford
1994	*Bradbury Star*	P. Hide	J. Gifford
1995	*Dublin Flyer*	B. Powell	Capt. T.A. Foster

MURPHY'S GOLD CUP

Year	Winner	Jockey	Trainer
1996	*Challenger Du Lac*	R. Dunwoody	M.C. Pipe

RITZ CLUB CHARITY TROPHY WINNERS

Each Festival the jockey who has the greatest number of wins during the Festival is awarded a trophy and a cheque is given to charity. This trophy was inaugurated in 1980.

Year	Trophy Winner	Number of wins
1980	A.J. Wilson	3
1981	J. Francome	3
1982	J.J. O'Neill	1
1983	G. Bradley	2
1984	J.J. O'Neill	2
1985	S. Smith-Eccles	3
1986	P. Scudamore	2
1987	P. Scudamore	2
1988	S. Sherwood	2
1989	T. Morgan	2
1990	R. Dunwoody	2
1991	P. Scudamore	2
1992	J. Osborne	5
1993	C. Swan	4
1994	C. Swan	3
1995	N. Williamson	4
1996	R. Dunwoody	2
1997	A. McCoy	3

Jim Wilson, the first winner of the Ritz Club Trophy, having just won the 1981 Gold Cup on *Little Owl*. *Little Owl* died in 1997.

ACKNOWLEDGEMENTS

I would like to express my most sincere thanks to the following people and institutions who helped me with material, advice and their own knowledge. Without them this book would never have been possible,

Of great importance was my sister, Jane, who came up with contacts and suggestions throughout the time I was working on this project.

I should like to thank photographers, Les Hurley and Terry Bliss who went to great pains to help me and provided many of the photographs that appear in this book – I am very indebted to their generosity,

For their time and willingness to talk to me I should particularly like to thank David Nicholson and his mother, Diana, Jim Wilson, Mrs Mercy Rimell, Mrs Joan Hamey, John Ryde and Mr and Mrs Owen O'Neill. I sincerely hope that this book meets with their approval.

For the invaluable loan of past results books, thanks are due to Mr Guy Olivotti.

My most heartfelt thanks also go to: Mr K. Blake, Dr S. Blake and the Cheltenham Art Gallery and Museum, Mr J. Cheeseman, all at the Cheltenham Library, Mr P. Dever, Mrs B. Elliott, Mr G. Excell, Mr W. Finch and the Gloucestershire Warwickshire Railway, Mr J. Fogarty and the Bakery Stores, Mr and Mrs R.A. Gill, Mrs Hankinson, Mr P. Jackson, Mr P. McNeile and the Cheltenham Racecourse, Mr R. Moss and the Royal Oak, Kinnersley, Mr S. O'Neill, Mr H. Osmond and Dean Close School, Mr B. Parkin, Mr T. Pearce and Cheltenham College, Mr P. Scudamore, Mr N. Smith, Mr R. Voysey, Mr I. Thompson, Mr M. Wilding and John Mowlem & Co. plc.

In some instances it has not been possible to ascertain the copyright holder of photographs. It is humbly hoped that any such omissions will be excused.

BRITAIN IN OLD PHOTOGRAPHS

Lincoln
Lincoln Cathedral
The Lincolnshire Coast
Liverpool
Around Llandudno
Around Lochaber
Theatrical London
Around Louth
The Lower Fal Estuary
Lowestoft
Luton
Lympne Airfield
Lytham St Annes
Maidenhead
Around Maidenhead
Around Malvern
Manchester
Manchester Road & Rail
Mansfield
Marlborough: A Second Selection
Marylebone & Paddington
Around Matlock
Melton Mowbray
Around Melksham
The Mendips
Merton & Morden
Middlesbrough
Midsomer Norton & Radstock
Around Mildenhall
Milton Keynes
Minehead
Monmouth & the River Wye
The Nadder Valley
Newark
Around Newark
Newbury
Newport, Isle of Wight
The Norfolk Broads
Norfolk at War
North Fylde
North Lambeth
North Walsham & District
Northallerton
Northampton
Around Norwich
Nottingham 1944–74
The Changing Face of Nottingham
Victorian Nottingham
Nottingham Yesterday & Today
Nuneaton
Around Oakham
Ormskirk & District
Otley & District
Oxford: The University
Oxford Yesterday & Today
Oxfordshire Railways: A Second
    Selection
Oxfordshire at School
Around Padstow
Pattingham & Wombourne

Penwith
Penzance & Newlyn
Around Pershore
Around Plymouth
Poole
Portsmouth
Poulton-le-Fylde
Preston
Prestwich
Pudsey
Radcliffe
RAF Chivenor
RAF Cosford
RAF Hawkinge
RAF Manston
RAF Manston: A Second Selection
RAF St Mawgan
RAF Tangmere
Ramsgate & Thanet Life
Reading
Reading: A Second Selection
Redditch & the Needle District
Redditch: A Second Selection
Richmond, Surrey
Rickmansworth
Around Ripley
The River Soar
Romney Marsh
Romney Marsh: A Second
    Selection
Rossendale
Around Rotherham
Rugby
Around Rugeley
Ruislip
Around Ryde
St Albans
St Andrews
Salford
Salisbury
Salisbury: A Second Selection
Salisbury: A Third Selection
Around Salisbury
Sandhurst & Crowthorne
Sandown & Shanklin
Sandwich
Scarborough
Scunthorpe
Seaton, Lyme Regis & Axminster
Around Seaton & Sidmouth
Sedgley & District
The Severn Vale
Sherwood Forest
Shrewsbury
Shrewsbury: A Second Selection
Shropshire Railways
Skegness
Around Skegness
Skipton & the Dales
Around Slough

Smethwick
Somerton & Langport
Southampton
Southend-on-Sea
Southport
Southwark
Southwell
Southwold to Aldeburgh
Stafford
Around Stafford
Staffordshire Railways
Around Staveley
Stepney
Stevenage
The History of Stilton Cheese
Stoke-on-Trent
Stoke Newington
Stonehouse to Painswick
Around Stony Stratford
Around Stony Stratford: A Second
    Selection
Stowmarket
Streatham
Stroud & the Five Valleys
Stroud & the Five Valleys: A
    Second Selection
Stroud's Golden Valley
The Stroudwater and Thames &
    Severn Canals
The Stroudwater and Thames &
    Severn Canals: A Second
    Selection
Suffolk at Work
Suffolk at Work: A Second
    Selection
The Heart of Suffolk
Sunderland
Sutton
Swansea
Swindon: A Third Selection
Swindon: A Fifth Selection
Around Tamworth
Taunton
Around Taunton
Teesdale
Teesdale: A Second Selection
Tenbury Wells
Around Tettenhall & Codshall
Tewkesbury & the Vale of
    Gloucester
Thame to Watlington
Around Thatcham
Around Thirsk
Thornbury to Berkeley
Tipton
Around Tonbridge
Trowbridge
Around Truro
TT Races
Tunbridge Wells

Tunbridge Wells: A Second
    Selection
Twickenham
Uley, Dursley & Cam
The Upper Fal
The Upper Tywi Valley
Uxbridge, Hillingdon & Cowley
The Vale of Belvoir
The Vale of Conway
Ventnor
Wakefield
Wallingford
Walsall
Waltham Abbey
Wandsworth at War
Wantage, Faringdon & the Vale
    Villages
Around Warwick
Weardale
Weardale: A Second Selection
Wednesbury
Wells
Welshpool
West Bromwich
West Wight
Weston-super-Mare
Around Weston-super-Mare
Weymouth & Portland
Around Wheatley
Around Whetstone
Whitchurch to Market Drayton
Around Whitstable
Wigton & the Solway Plain
Willesden
Around Wilton
Wimbledon
Around Windsor
Wingham, Addisham &
    Littlebourne
Wisbech
Witham & District
Witney
Around Witney
The Witney District
Wokingham
Around Woodbridge
Around Woodstock
Woolwich
Woolwich Royal Arsenal
Around Wootton Bassett,
    Cricklade & Purton
Worcester
Worcester in a Day
Around Worcester
Worcestershire at Work
Around Worthing
Wotton-under-Edge to Chipping
    Sodbury
Wymondham & Attleborough
The Yorkshire Wolds

To order any of these titles please telephone our distributor, Littlehampton Book Services on 01903 721596
For a catalogue of these and our other titles please ring Regina Schinner on 01453 731114